Creation
& Evolution
101

Bruce BICKEL
&
Stan JANTZ

HARVEST HOUSE PUBLISHERS

EUGENE, OREGON

Cover by Left Coast Design, Portland, Oregon

CREATION AND EVOLUTION 101
Formerly titled *Bruce & Stan's® Guide to How It All Began*
Copyright © 2001 by Bruce Bickel and Stan Jantz
Published by Harvest House Publishers
Eugene, Oregon 97402
www.harvesthousepublishers.com

Library of Congress Cataloging-in-Publication Data
Bickel, Bruce, 1952-
  Creation and evolution 101 / Bruce Bickel and Stan Jantz.
    p. cm.—(Christianity 101)
Rev. ed. of: Bruce & Stan's guide to how it all began.
Includes bibliographical references and index.
    ISBN 0-7369-1060-3 (pbk.)
1. Creation. 2. Evolution—Religious aspects—Christianity. I. Title: Creation and evolution one hundred and one. II. Title: Creation and evolution one hundred one. III. Jantz, Stan, 1952– IV. Bickel, Bruce, 1952– Bruce & Stan's guide to how it all began. V. Title. VI. Series.
  BT695.B46 2004
  231.7'65—dc21   2003020329

Printed in the United States of America

04 05 06 07 08 09 10 11 12 / BP-KB / 10 9 8 7 6 5 4 3 2 1

Contents

Part I: In the Beginning

Part II: God Created the Heavens and the Earth

Part III: And God Saw That It Was Good

About the Authors

Bruce Bickel wasn't very successful as a stand-up comic, so he became a lawyer (and more people laugh at him now). He is a keynote speaker on management ethics at corporate events and speaks frequently at churches and Christian conferences. Bruce resides in Fresno, California, with his wife, Cheryl.

Stan Jantz managed a chain of Christian retail stores for more than 25 years. Currently, he is a marketing consultant and a partner in a community-building software company. Stan and his wife, Karin, live in Southern California.

Bruce & Stan have cowritten 45 books with more than 2 million copies sold.

About Our Science Adviser

John Wiester is the chairman of the Science Education Commission of the American Scientific Affiliation (ASA), an association of Christians in the sciences headquartered in Ipswich, Massachusetts. He has taught the geology course at Biola University, and for the past five years he has taught the origins course at Westmont College, where he serves as adjunct instructor of biology. Wiester is coauthor of *What's Darwin Got to Do with It: A Friendly Conversation About Evolution* (InterVarsity Press). He is also coauthor of the ASA book for high school science teachers, *Teaching Science in a Climate of Controversy*. He has also written numerous articles for the ASA journal, *Perspectives*. His most recent articles include "Paradigm Shifts in Geology and Biology: Geosynclinal Theory and Plate Tectonics" and "Darwinism and Intelligent Design."

A Note from the Authors

We're not afraid of a little intellectual controversy. Actually, we think that it is good from time to time because it gets people thinking (just so long as they stop short of strangling each other). We wrote about a rather controversial subject in our book *Bruce & Stan's Guide to Bible Prophecy*. We enjoyed writing about the differing viewpoints, and our readers apparently liked our approach of presenting the information (and the opposing views) without a lot of shouting and finger wagging. (Okay, we know that it is impossible to shout and finger wag in a book, but you get our point.)

Since we have already covered how the world will end, we thought we ought to write about how the world got started. (Most people would tackle these topics in chronological order, but not us. We consider ourselves to be contrarians. Of course, other people just think that we are backward.) Anyway, we're ready to jump back into the bubbling pot of controversy with this book on how the world began. We think you'll find this subject fascinating. We sure did. And even though there is a huge hullabaloo about these issues (involving the Bible, science, and philosophy), the whole debate can be reduced to some fairly simple and straightforward positions. And as we have done with our other books, we'll just lay out for you the basics of each viewpoint. (In other words, we're sticking with that "no shouting, no finger wagging" approach.)

We discovered something very interesting in writing this book: In some ways, knowing how the world began is even more important than knowing how it will end. Does that surprise you? It did us. We think you'll discover the same thing. It all has to do with understanding that God has a master plan for the world and a specific plan for you. Here is what God had to say about it:

> *"For I know the plans I have for you," says the* LORD.
> *"They are plans for good and not for disaster, to give you*
> *a future and a hope....If you look for me in earnest, you*

will find me....I will be found by you," says the LORD
(Jeremiah 29:11-14).

We are convinced that if you study the evidence of how the
world began, you'll realize that God considers you to be a very
special part of it. Whether you're looking in a microscope or
through a telescope, you can see evidence of God's grand design.
You are a part of it, but you'll get a better perspective if you step
back—way back—before the world began. (Trust us. Even from
way back there, you'll be able to see yourself and how you fit into
it all.)

Introduction

*I*f you are like many people, you are fascinated about the beginning of the world:

- You're intrigued by the magnitude of the galaxies.

- You're curious about archaeological discoveries of dinosaur fossils and caveman skeletons.

- You wonder if we are alone in the universe or if there are signs of intelligent life on other planets (because intelligent life seems pretty difficult to find on *this* one).

But...

- You're intimidated because you haven't studied science since that unfortunate explosion in the classroom lab (which they still haven't been able to pin on you), so you feel like you are working with information that is out-of-date.

- If you don't believe in evolution, you're afraid that you'll end up getting into a debate that you're sure to lose because everyone talks like it is an undeniable fact.

- The PBS programs say that the earth is billions of years old, but you've seen a genealogical chart of the generations of people from the Old Testament that calculated that

Adam lived about 6000 years ago (which would make the earth about 6000 years and five days old, according to the Bible's Creation story in Genesis). You want to believe the Bible, but you know better than to expose yourself to ridicule for contradicting PBS.

So whenever there is talk about the beginning of the world or the origin of the human race, you just sit still with one hand over your mouth, one hand over each of your eyes, and one hand over each of your ears (this assumes you can borrow several hands from people standing nearby).

But wait! It doesn't have to be like that. You don't have to be afraid or intimidated anymore. We know from personal experience.

What This Book Is All About

We don't blame you for being a little hesitant to explore the "beginning of the world" issues. After all, these issues are at the heart of several very heated (and sometimes hostile) debates. Think of it as kind of a World Wrestling Entertainment Grudge match. (The emotions and adrenaline are just as high, but there is a lot less sweat and fewer body slams.) Here are the contestants in the great "Creation vs. Evolution" debate:

- In the "Creation" corner, you've got the people who believe that God created the universe, the earth, and the human race in six 24-hour days, as some interpret chapter 1 of Genesis. These people believe the earth is 6000 to 10,000 years old (according to Adam's family tree).

- In the "Evolution" corner, you've got the people who believe that it all just happened by chance. They state that the universe is billions and billions of years old, and that during that time frame all of life just fell into place by random happenstance. They reject the notion that God (or any type of outside intelligence) was involved in the process.

- And hopping into the ring is a relatively new contestant: a group of scientists who dispute the other two viewpoints. They agree that the universe and earth are billions of years old, but they find too much complexity and order in the world (and its inhabitants) for all of it to have happened by chance. They are persuaded that there must be some intelligent designer behind it all.

Well, we are generalizing, of course. The wrestling match analogy isn't perfect. There are some further deviations and distinctions. But you get our drift. With all these opposing opinions and theories, it is difficult to sort it all out.

That's where we come in. We're kind of like the referees in the great origins debate. We're not up to actually competing in the ring with these scientific and philosophical heavyweights. So we won't fight with them, but we *can* keep them separated long enough for you to figure out who they are and what they stand for. Then you can decide for yourself who to believe.

What You'll Find Inside

You can already tell that this isn't a typical science textbook. (Very few of them ever make a reference to professional wrestling.) And if it were a science textbook, you probably wouldn't have started reading it in the first place. But you'll find a lot of science in it. We've got chapters on:

- *Cosmology*. This has nothing to do with women's makeup or hairstyles, but it does have everything to do with the cosmos. We'll be examining facts and theories about how the universe was formed and its characteristics. Very recent discoveries in outer space have profound implications for determining whether the universe was created at some point in the past or whether it has always existed.

- *Astronomy*. No, we won't be talking about your horoscope. That's astrology. Astronomy is the fascinating study of stars and planets. You see, the size, position, and motion of the planets in our solar system all have significant impact on life on Earth.

- *Geology*. Geology is more than just the study of dirt and rocks. Maybe this subject caused you to doze off in elementary school, but we think you'll be amazed with what you'll learn about the structure and composition of the earth. There is a lot of shifting going on, and we think it will keep you wide awake. (Just ask any Californian.)

- *Archaeology*. In several chapters, we'll be looking at famous old fossils. No, we aren't talking about Joan Rivers or Dick Clark. Think older than that. We'll be looking at fossils from dinosaurs. And our study of archaeology will have us talking about cavemen, too. (And aren't these two subjects the ones that puzzle you the most about the history of the world and the human race?)

- *Biology*. Your last experience with biology was probably examining the guts of a frog you were dissecting in the tenth grade. Our review of the characteristics of plants and animals will be much more interesting than frog innards (and you won't be bothered by the stench of formaldehyde).

But this isn't just a book about science. Science might give us clues for the "Where did I come from?" and the "How did I get here?" questions. But those aren't the only questions that have been pestering mankind. The investigation of our origins also leads us to the study of:

- *Philosophy*. Much of the discussion of origins involves scientific *theories*. Some of them can be supported by factual evidence; others cannot. We think you'll agree with us that a theory shouldn't be believed just because some person in a white lab coat proclaimed it. Logic and reason play a big part in analyzing the origins of the universe and life within it. And if you are the least bit skeptical (as we tend to be), then you may suspect that some of the so-called scientific theories about origins were merely concocted to support someone's personal philosophy.

- *Theology*. Religion had explanations for how the world began long before there were scientists. And we certainly cannot discuss the subject of origins without including God. After all, so much of the debate is about Him. Well, not so much Him personally, but whether He was involved in the process of bringing the world and life into existence. Questions naturally arise: Does the Bible know more than science? Does science prove the Bible is wrong? Since the Bible proclaims itself to be true, and since it addresses the subject of how all things began, it needs to be investigated.

We hope we are conveying that this book covers some pretty heavy subjects. It does! But don't think you'll need to be an astrophysicist or an archbishop to understand it. There are plenty of books written for these types. But this book is for those of us who have a life outside the laboratory or the monastery. Here's the approach we will be taking with this book:

- *Correct*. Above all else, we want to give you correct information. We haven't made stuff up or hidden information that doesn't agree with our personal viewpoints. As you will find out, this book includes a lot about science and a lot about the Bible. We were able to handle the Bible stuff fairly well, but worried that we would be a little weak on the science end of it. (Don't let that concern you. If we had been science geniuses, then we would have written one of those complicated textbooks that you wouldn't be reading anyway.) Realizing our deficiencies in the scientific realm, we researched the subject of origins for several years. We read those thick textbooks that you have probably ignored. And to make sure that we summarized the viewpoints, theories, and factual evidence correctly (and to make sure we weren't confusing ourselves), we asked Professor John Wiester to serve as our science adviser on this book. (The analogy of a guide dog for the blind comes to mind.) Anyway, we have done our best to give you current and accurate information.

- *Clear*. The resource books we read were very helpful, but it took a long time to read them. Not only were they lengthy, but we often had to read each line about three times. Sometimes the scientific and theological terminology can obfuscate the meaning for the lay reader. Not so with this book. We won't use big words just for the sake of trying to impress you (like we did with *obfuscate*). Be assured that if we have to use complicated terminology, we'll explain it for you (*obfuscate:* to make something so confusing that it is difficult to understand).

- *Casual.* We've had a fun time writing this book, and we hope you have an enjoyable time reading it. The subjects are serious, but that doesn't mean you have to read the book with a furrowed brow. We find quite a bit of humor in the way some people deal with the idea of God when examining the origins of life and the universe. We can promise you we won't be stuffy because, hey, we aren't trying to impress you with how amazing we are. (You'll be sufficiently impressed with the amazing facts of how the world began.)

Why You Need to Read This Book

You need to read this book even if you haven't had a burning curiosity about how the world began. Why? We're glad you asked.

What you decide about how the world began affects your view of the world (in general) and yourself (in particular). Here's what we mean: If life just happened by chance, then there is no significance to any of it; it is meaningless. But if there was some higher power that put all of life into place, then we might want to find out more about the plans of that higher power.

So, what we decide about our origins may tell us a lot about our life right now. And finding out how it all began might give us clues to how life ends, and if there is life after death. Therefore, learning about how the universe and life began is not just an intellectual exercise—it is a way to discover the meaning of what life is all about.

This Book Is for You If...

Maybe you are not really struggling with the huge philosophical and theological questions about your place in the universe.

Maybe you just want some simple answers to some basic questions. Either way, we think you'll find what you're looking for in this book. But if you need a little more assurance, we think this book will be perfect for you if...

- You just want to know why the Bible never mentions dinosaurs.

- You are curious about whether a "day" of Creation in Genesis chapter 1 is 24 hours long or longer.

- Your brother-in-law has one of those car decals of a Darwin fish with feet. You don't really believe in evolution, but he talks like it is an established fact. You would like to know if there are any fallacies in the theory of evolution because you need some arguments to use against him.

- You are skeptical about the biblical account of Creation. All of that happening in six days seems a little too much to believe. You are wondering how intelligent people could possibly swallow the Creation story.

- You believe the Bible's account of Creation, but everyone seems to think that it is contradicted by science. If there is any scientific evidence that supports the Bible, you are anxious to hear it.

- You are wondering if the big bang theory contradicts the Bible.

- You have children, and you need some information you can use to explain to them how the world began (and you haven't been paying much attention to scientific discoveries since John Glenn went into space—the first time).

- You're a kid, and you know all the technical stuff. But you need a little help figuring out how to say it in a simplified, basic "dummies" fashion so you can explain it to your parents.

- You only have one question: What is life all about? You have gone to all of the usual places for answers (school,

MTV, church, Oprah), but so far you've got diddly-squat. You are still searching.

If you are in any of these categories or close to them, then this book is for you. We've had very similar questions, and we'll share with you the information that we found. (Notice that we didn't say that we'll give you the answers. We'll give you some good information, and you can make the decisions for yourself. Wouldn't you really rather have it that way?)

How to Use This Book

We recognize that each reader has a personal reading style. We designed this book for you to read from the beginning to the end (what a unique approach!), but you don't have to do it that way. You can skip around. We won't be offended. Some of you may be speed-readers, while others may be plodders. (Aah, we can smell the odor of yellow highlighter pen already.) Here are a couple other suggestions:

1. **We've got questions.** At the end of every chapter, we've included some questions. These aren't "true or false" or "yes or no" type of inquires. And they aren't multiple choice. These questions are designed to help you think through what you read and make some personal application of it.

2. **Get in a group.** You might want to study this book together with other people. There will be plenty of topics that should generate stimulating conversation and debate. Maybe someone else's opinion will help you formulate your own, or vice versa. If you are a leader of such a group, don't worry about how to get the discussion going; that's what the questions at the end of the book are for.

3. **Visit us online.** We have an interactive online resource exclusively for readers of *Creation and Evolution 101* and other books in the Christianity 101 series. Click on www.christianity101online.com. There you will find a

number of features designed to help you learn even more about the subjects of this book. See the details at the back of this book.

Enough of this preliminary stuff. Let's dive right into a lively discussion about how the world began. We'll be talking about the beginning, but we'll also be talking about whether there was anything before the beginning.

Part I
In the Beginning

*C*hapter 1

Something began me and it had no
beginning: something will end me and it
has no end.

—*Carl Sandburg*

Here's a fun little quiz. We're going to give you some famous "first lines." See if you can guess where they came from:

"Call me Ishmael." _____
    (Hint: it's from a book about a very big whale.)

"Four score and seven years ago…" _____
    (Hint: This first line was in a speech written on the back of an envelope. Second hint: The guy who wrote it had a mole.)

"We called him Old Yeller." _____
    (Hint: The title of the book is in the first line. Second hint: The name of the dog is in the first line. Third hint: The dog dies in the end.)

How are you doing so far? Here's one more for extra credit:

    "In the beginning God created the heavens and the earth." _____
    (Hint: It's from the bestselling book in the world. Second hint: It's what *Knowing the Bible 101* is all about. Third hint: There are no more hints.)

First lines are important to books, speeches, and even the Bible (oops, we gave away one of the answers). They're important because they set the tone for the beginning of the story or the point you're trying to get across. The first line of the Bible is there because it sets the tone for the rest of the story. Without the Bible's first line, "In the beginning…" and the important information that follows, we wouldn't know where we came from, why we're here, what we're supposed to do, or where we're going.

Are we stretching things just a bit? We don't think so. As you read this book, we think you're going to see for yourself exactly what we mean.

Why Begin at the Beginning?

It was a bright and beautiful morning, and there we were touring the campus of the University of California at Berkeley, just across the bay from San Francisco. It didn't take us long to figure out that we were probably the dumbest guys walking through Sather Gate on this particular day. We knew this because, when it comes to academics, Cal (as it is known by locals and students alike) just happens to be the number one public university in the country. And it's one of the leading universities in the world when it comes to science.

The way we figured it, our *combined* SAT scores didn't equal the *average* SAT scores of the Cal students. We were way out of our league. So what were we doing at Cal?

We made the trek to Berkeley for *you!* Sure, we had read and scoured dozens of complicated books in order to write this one simple one, but we wanted to go one step further. We wanted to talk to some living, breathing scientists about the subject of this book, just to make sure we had the latest information. So we contacted some highly respected science professors at Cal and asked if we could interview them.

(This is where being dumb has its advantages. The smart students are generally intimidated by their even smarter professors, but not us. We just called these guys and asked if we could talk to them about science and what it means to average people like us, and they said, "Why not? Come on over, and bring a sandwich while you're at it.")

The Three Professors

We want to tell you the story of our day at Cal and our conversation with three different professors. All of them are world-renowned (that means they're famous in the scientific community, even though you'll never read about them in *People* magazine). We sat down with each one in his office and had a meaningful dialogue. (Okay, so they talked and we listened, but we did a good job of listening and saying stuff like "Uh-huh" and "Really?") We asked each of them about the beginning of the universe, and not just because it's the topic of this book. This is a topic that has turned the scientific community on its collective ear. And it is already impacting the way everyone else views the world.

We may not be experts, but we do know this: Science has made incredible discoveries in the last few decades—and particularly in the last few years—that verify what the Bible has said all along about how it all began.

"The evidence is incontrovertible."

The first professor we talked to teaches astronomy and physics at Cal. He was smart and personable, and he got very animated when he talked about the universe and how it began. "The evidence for the beginning of the universe is incontrovertible," he said, gesturing broadly. (Note: We promised not to use big words like *incontrovertible,* but we can't be responsible for what really smart astronomers say. As a public service, we looked up the word. It means "cannot be disputed...too clear to be argued about." This was a big relief to us. We thought the word meant "unable to lower the top on your sports car.")

He had more to say. "We know what happened in the first three minutes of the universe's beginning. Now we're working on the first second."

"We are the first generation in history to see this."

We went to the second professor's office, which is located in the Lawrence Berkeley Lab (trust us, this is a very impressive building because of what goes on inside). This particular guy, who is an astrophysicist, was the leader of a science project that measured the beginning of the universe (this was a *very big* science project, not like your sixth grade science-fair entry that measured the mold on a block of cheese).

"We are the first generation in history to see this," he said.

"See what?" we asked, trying to look intelligent.

"The beginning of the universe," he replied.

"You have seen the beginning of the universe?"

"Oh yes. We've measured the effects of the beginning. We have found evidence for the birth of the universe. No one has ever done this before."

Our minds were spinning. We thanked our second professor and left, suddenly hungry for some cheese.

"I see a time when science and religion will come together."

The third professor we interviewed at Cal was a Nobel prize laureate (he was awarded the prize for his work in infrared astronomy). Because of his impeccable credentials, we asked him the burning question you may be asking right now: "If we now know that the universe had a beginning, what are the implications?" Or to put it another way, "What does this mean?"

Our Nobel prize friend didn't hesitate at all. "Science exists to tell us how the universe works," he explained. "Religion exists to tell us what it means. There's no question in my mind that science and religion are going to come together in the future to give us the answers we are looking for." (Note: You won't have to wait any longer than the end of this chapter to find out.)

So What Does This Mean?

We were pretty excited when we left Cal that day. We had just met with some of the top scientists in the world, and they were basically telling us what we want to tell you in this book:

- *"The evidence is incontrovertible."* It's not often that you'll hear a scientist say this (it was our first time), but it happens. Sir Isaac Newton said it about gravity after the apple hit him on the noggin. Ben Franklin was convinced that electricity existed when he flew his kite. And now scientists are absolutely certain that the evidence points to a clear and simple fact: The universe had a beginning.

  We're going to talk about the evidence for the beginning of the universe and beyond in Part Two, but right here at the beginning of the book we want to assure you that scientists working today do not dispute this fact.

- *"We are the first generation to see this."* Before the twentieth century, scientists pretty much believed that the universe was eternal. In other words, they believed it has always been here and would be here forever. There was no real evidence for this scientific assertion, but that's what most scientists believed. But it contradicted the Bible, which clearly states, "In the beginning God created the heavens and the earth." Therefore, science and religion seemed completely separate and completely incompatible.

  Then at the beginning of the twentieth century, a series of scientific discoveries pointed to a much different picture. In 1922, physicist Richard Tolman recognized that the universe is expanding, not holding steady or oscillating endlessly. Between 1929 and 1936, astronomer Edwin Hubble peered through his 100-inch telescope and proved the same thing.

But it wasn't until the late twentieth century—in your lifetime—that scientists working on the Cosmic Background Explorer satellite (COBE) confirmed what Tolman and Hubble and many others were saying: The universe began with a simple, incredibly powerful event scientists call "the big bang."

We cannot overemphasize the importance of this discovery, which Stephen Hawking called "the discovery of the century." For thousands of years people have wondered about how it all began. If they didn't believe the Bible, all they had to go on was scientific theory. If they believed the Bible, then they worried that it was impossible to verify what it was saying.

The First First

No doubt you have seen a lot of "firsts" in your life. Some have been good firsts—like the first time you drove a car, and some not-so-good—like your first ticket. But this "first"—the first conclusive evidence for the beginning of the universe—has to be at the top of your list of firsts.

Why? Because if there is a beginning, there has to be a Beginner. If there is an origin, there has to be an Originator. It's that simple. A lot of scientists and nonscientists alike are still struggling with the implications of "the discovery of the century." Many have come to the "incontrovertible" conclusion that there's something or someone beyond the universe that got everything going.

- *"Science and religion will come together."* Our third professor friend was the oldest of the three, and in our opinion he was the wisest (there's something about wisdom and age that go together). He understood the implications of all this stuff we've been talking about. He understood that science can only tell us how things work.

It can't explain what it means. That's the role of philosophy and religion.

As the professor stated, there's no reason why science and religion can't come together. We would like to take it one step further and say there's no reason why science can't come together with a belief in God and the Bible.

Science is neither good nor bad in itself. It simply observes the universe and measures what's in it—temperature, time, speed, weight, frequency, etc. Scientists try to find out if the measurements are consistent or repeatable, and then they come to conclusions based on the evidence. Such scientific truth will never contradict the truth about God.

So there's no reason why people who believe in God should fear science or worry that scientists are out to undermine their faith, as long as the scientists are really seeking truth and not just trying to find proof for their preexisting beliefs. If the history of science tells us anything, it's this: The more we learn about how the universe began and how it works, the more the universe points to God.

King David, who lived 3000 years ago, loved God and was very interested in science. Here's what he wrote:

> The heavens tell of the glory of God. The skies display his marvelous craftsmanship. Day after day they continue to speak; night after night they make him known (Psalm 19:1-2).

Why Is the Beginning So Important?

Yes, science has proven beyond any doubt that the universe had a beginning at a specific point in time, but this is a fairly recent discovery for the science community in particular, and to the rest of the world in general. It's true! The idea that the universe had a specific beginning has never been widely accepted, except by those who believe in the Bible. Philosophers and scientists alike have resisted this notion because of the *huge* implications we have already talked about.

---

*I*f the universe had a beginning, then something external to the universe must have caused it to come into existence—something, or Someone, transcendent to the natural world. As a result, the idea of creation is no longer merely a matter of religious faith; it is a conclusion based on the most straightforward reading of the scientific evidence.

—Charles Colson

You can understand why some people would be so resistant to the evidence that the universe has a beginning. Okay, let's play that game for a moment. Let's look at the other side of the debate and say that the universe didn't have a beginning. What are your options? We can think of three:

1. **The universe doesn't exist.** Don't laugh. This has to be one of the options to a universe without a beginning: It doesn't exist. But it's a lousy option. It is impossible for the universe *not* to exist because, by its very definition, "the universe includes everything that exists" (that's straight from the *Oxford English Dictionary*). Since it contains everything that exists, the universe also must exist. Here's another angle. If the universe doesn't exist, then nothing else exists either, and the whole issue doesn't matter.

2. **The universe has always existed.** We have already referred to this option. A lot of scientists throughout history have believed that the universe has always existed in a "steady state." This idea has also been known as the "continuous creation theory," and it goes something like this: The universe had no beginning, but rather existed in a steady-state condition with new matter being formed from that which was already there.

   According to this theory, the universe has existed in this way throughout all time. The ancient Greeks believed this idea. In the eighteenth century, scientists believed that matter could neither be created nor destroyed. Christian commentator Charles Colson writes that this theory "became a potent weapon in the hands of the ardent materialists, who argued that science itself now ruled out any ultimate creation."

Well, you may still hear about a scientist here and there who will argue for the steady-state universe, but he will only be doing so because he refuses to accept the profound implications that the universe had a beginning and therefore is not the ultimate reality.

3. The universe created itself. You used to hear the term *spontaneous generation*. This is what option three is all about. It means that the universe and everything in it appeared as if by accident. There was no reason or explanation for this appearing of the universe; it "just happened."

The problem with this theory is that it violates all laws (scientific or otherwise) of logic, reason, and common sense. The first law of thermodynamics (the conservation of matter) says that matter cannot just come into existence. In other words, matter cannot create itself. The second law of thermodynamics (the decay of matter) says that the universe and everything in it is in the constant process of disintegration. In other words, matter does not last forever.

If the laws of physics aren't enough to convince you, then how about a Latin lesson? Here's a little phrase you can use to impress your friends at parties: *Ex nihilo, nihil fit.* That means, "From nothing, nothing comes." If you have nothing to begin with, you can't get something. All you get is more nothing.

The Fourth Possibility

But the universe had to come from somewhere. If it exists now, and it hasn't always existed, and it didn't create itself, then where did it come from? There is only one other possibility, which we are calling the fourth possibility (aren't we clever?).

Here's how it goes: If there is a beginning, there had to be a Beginner. If there is a universe, something or someone had to cause it. This is called the principle of cause and effect, which goes like this: Every effect has a cause. The universe is an *effect,* and therefore it must have a cause. Simple as that.

If an effect doesn't have a cause, then you are back to our first three possibilities: The effect doesn't exist, the effect has always existed, or the effect created itself. This is true whether you are talking about the universe, yourself, or the most beautiful car you can think of (we're thinking of a Ferrari). The universe didn't just appear, you didn't just appear, and the Ferrari didn't just appear. There had to be a cause of some kind.

The First Big Cause

We think we've made our point, but just in case you missed it, here it is again: Everything in the universe has a cause. But there's something else to think about. As you go back further and further in the "chain of causes," you must eventually come to a First Cause that got the whole thing going. Without the First Cause (which we like to call the First Big Cause), nothing else (including you) would exist.

Without a First Big Cause, you would have nothing to begin with, which means all of the other causes in the universe wouldn't exist either. But because we have a universe, there must have been something there before the universe existed that caused the universe to exist (isn't this fun?).

Fred Heeren, a respected science writer, put it this way in his book *Show Me God:* "A series of causes cannot be infinite. There must have been a first cause, which itself is uncaused."

Another way to say it is this: The First Big Cause had to be *self-existent.* In other words, it had to always exist. And if something had to be self-existent, then what or who is it? To put it another way, what or who is the First Big Cause?

So What or Who Is the First Big Cause?

We thought you would never ask. When it comes to the First Big Cause, there are only two choices:

Choice #1—The universe is the First Big Cause.

Choice #2—God is the First Big Cause.

There are no other choices. These are the only two you get (if you think you have some other viable alternatives, we would like to hear them! You can e-mail us at info@twelvetwomedia.com). Let's take a look at each choice.

No Such Thing as Chance

One of the choices you might be thinking about for the First Big Cause is "chance." It goes something like this: *The universe came about by chance.* This really isn't a choice at all, because chance can't cause anything. Only a real force is capable of causation, and chance can't cause anything because it isn't a real force. The philosopher David Hume wrote, "It is universally allowed that nothing exists without a cause of its existence, and that chance, when strictly examined, is a mere negative word, and means not any real power which has anywhere a being in nature."

The Universe Is the First Big Cause

Okay, we've already been over this ground. We have already said that the universe can't create itself, and it can't cause itself either. The universe can cause all kinds of other effects, but by itself the universe can't be a cause. Something else outside the universe had to cause the universe.

The word *universe* comes from two different words—*unity* and *diversity*—that are blended into one.

God Is the First Big Cause

Since the universe can't be the First Big Cause, then we are left with only one other choice. God is the First Big Cause. In his book

Not a Chance, R. C. Sproul writes that "there must be a self-existent being of some sort somewhere, or nothing would or could exist. A self-existent being is both logically and ontologically necessary."

By "ontologically necessary," Dr. Sproul means that there must be a self-existent being in order for anything else to exist. This being must be eternal, and it must have no "antecedent cause," or else it would be dependent on something else for its existence.

$\mathcal{B}$ut Who Made God?

People often make the mistake of assuming that for God to exist, God had to be made. Wrong! Just the opposite is true. For an eternal, infinite, all-powerful, all-knowing God to exist, He must not have a cause. He must not be an effect. R. C. Sproul writes:

A self-existent, eternal being exists by its own intrinsic power of being. It is dependent on nothing outside itself for its own being. Since it exists by its own eternal power of being, it is altogether underived, independent, and invulnerable to anything outside itself.

God has no beginning and therefore no cause. He has always been and He will always be. God does not need outside support to exist. This is what is meant by *self-existent.* King David understood this when he wrote:

Before the mountains were created, before you made the earth and the world, you are God, without beginning or end (Psalm 90:2).

Why Does God Have to Be the First Big Cause?

Recently we were listening to a talk show where the subject was God (He gets a lot of attention these days). A man called in, and he was mad. He said it was ridiculous to believe in God, and that it wasn't us humans who needed God, but just the opposite. "God needs us more than we need God."

What this caller was implying was that humankind is the center of the universe, we are the products of an endless process of evolution, and someday we are going to evolve into perfect beings. Meanwhile, we invented God for our own convenience.

God can pretty much be who we want Him to be. Without us, He wouldn't exist.

You don't hear many people express their views about God this openly, but a lot of people think this way. They believe in God, but He is a fairy-tale God. He is a God with human qualities and human frailties, and He exists only because we think about Him. When you confront these same people with the undeniable evidence that there had to be a First Big Cause, they respond by saying, "Why do you have to call this higher power God? Why can't we call it *Mother Earth* or the *Cosmic Being?*"

God Is

There's a very good reason why the great Beginner, the original Originator, and the First Big Cause is God. Because God is. He isn't our invention. He isn't an abstract concept. God is, and above Him there is no other. God exists apart from us, but we do not exist apart from Him. We didn't invent Him. The only reason we can think about God in the first place is because He put those thoughts into our very beings (Romans 1:19-20).

In the next chapter, we're going to talk more about God and His amazing personality traits. You're going to see that the word God means much more than "self-existent" and "eternal." You're going to see that God is a personal Being who has communicated with us in a profound and personal way.

---

*T*he word God...indicates a holy and personal being who is worthy of worship and to whom all persons are held ultimately accountable.

—R. C. Sproul

But don't take our word for it. Read what God says about Himself in the Bible, His personal message to all humankind:

I Am the One Who Always Is (Exodus 3:14).

Do you want to get to know God better? Do you want to know how He brought this incredible universe into existence? Then keep reading. The best is yet to come!

"What's That Again?"

1. The evidence for the beginning of the universe is incontrovertible. That means it is beyond dispute.

2. Science tells us how the universe works, and religion tells us what it means.

3. Since the universe exists, and the universe cannot cause itself, it must have a cause outside itself, which we call the First Big Cause.

4. Only God can be the First Big Cause, because only God is self-existent and eternal.

5. God doesn't exist because we invented Him. God exists because God is.

Dig Deeper

One of our favorite authors is also one of the smartest we know. Dr. Hugh Ross is an astrophysicist who has written several books on the Creator and the cosmos. In fact, that's the first one we recommend you read: *The Creator and the Cosmos.* In it Dr. Ross shows how "the greatest scientific discoveries of the century" reveal God.

We also like R. C. Sproul, our favorite theologian. His book *Not a Chance* takes you step-by-step through the rational explanation for a personal God.

Charles Colson writes with passion and authority about the issues facing all of us in our world. In his book *How Now Shall We Live?,* Colson grapples with the importance of an integrated worldview that includes God. His chapters on origins are worth the price of the book.

■ ■ ■

Questions for Reflection and Discussion

1. When respected scientists say the evidence for the beginning of the universe is incontrovertible, what implications does this have for the rest of the scientific community?

2. Why do you think we are the first generation to scientifically prove that our universe had a beginning? Why did this discovery occur at this time in history? How does this affect the way you think about the universe, as well as the way you think about your life?

3. Do you think it is important that science and a belief in God come together? Do you think this will happen in your lifetime? What if it never happens? How would this impact your beliefs?

4. Review the three options for a universe without a beginning. Which of these has been most prevalent in our culture? Why have scientists been so eager to explain away a definite beginning? Why is it so important that the Bible begins with Genesis 1:1?

5. Reflect on this statement: "In order for an eternal, infinite, all-powerful, all-knowing God to exist, He must not have a cause." What would God be like if He were caused or created? Why must God be self-existent?

6. What if the universe didn't exist? Would God still exist? Why? List at least two reasons why you think God created the universe in the first place.

■ ■ ■

Moving On...

As we said in the Introduction, your view of how the world began shapes your view of the world and yourself. Hey, we're not the first ones to think about this incredibly meaningful idea. At the end of his popular book *A Brief History of Time*, Stephen Hawking posed the following questions: "What is the nature of the universe? What is our place in it and where did we come from? Why is it the way it is?" Syndicated columnist Ellen Goodman wrote, "The anxiety about the *origins* of human life is really anxiety about the *meaning* of human life."

If this stuff is new to you, then we congratulate you for hanging in there this long (even though we just finished chapter 1). What that tells us is that you desire to know the truth. If you are simply reviewing the basics about God and the beginning of the universe, then we hope you're learning some new stuff that will be useful as you talk to your friends and family about your faith.

Either way, it's important that you know what you believe. Dr. Ravi Zacharias says that every person should have a worldview that makes sense, and this worldview should be able to answer questions related to these four things:

- *origins*

- *meaning*

- *morality*

- *destiny*

Our job in *Creation and Evolution 101* is to help you answer the questions about origins and meaning. We hope we're off to a good start.

*C*hapter 2

> What is the ultimate solution to the origin of the Universe? The answers provided by the astronomers are disconcerting and remarkable. Most remarkable of all is the fact that in science, as in the Bible, the world begins with an act of creation.
>
> —*astronomer Robert Jastrow*

When you boil it all down, either there was some sort of divine being involved with the beginning of the universe, or there wasn't. It is really that simple. There are just these two mutually exclusive alternatives: God or no God.

Well, we've got to start somewhere, so in this chapter we are going to look at the origins of the universe as if God created them. (We'll get to the "no God" alternative in chapter 3.)

Now, you might be wondering which "God" we're going to be talking about. After all, with so many different religions in the world, there are quite a few diverse concepts of "God" floating around. Well, we're going to be talking about the God of the Bible. (Don't go leaping to any conclusions that we are narrow-minded, intolerant, or prejudiced against other religions. We'll also explain why we are using the Bible as our resource.)

Don't just blow through this chapter thinking that you know it all because you sat through some Sunday school classes when you were a kid. You'll need to know what we say in this chapter to fully understand the big debate that we discuss in chapter 3. So speed-read it if you must, but don't skip it.

The Story of God

*B*ack in chapter 1, we were laying Latin and logic on you (which may be the reason you put this book down for a while). We're sorry about that, but you've got to admit that it made some sense:

- The Latin: *Ex nihilo nihil fit* (verbatim translation: "From nothing, nothing comes"). Our translation: "Somethin' doesn't come from nothin'."

- The logic: There is a cause for every effect. The universe is a very big effect. Therefore, there must have been a very big cause.

Okay, that was the easy part. Now let's try to get a handle on what (or who) could be the First Big Cause that started the universe.

Looking at the Profile of the First Big Cause

We can get some very precise and descriptive clues about the First Big Cause by examining the universe itself. Just like a police sketch artist, we can start to draw a picture of what the First Big Cause looks like from those clues. Of course, the universe tends to speak in rather scientific terms, so we'll need to engage the services of a translator. That's where we found the writings of Fred Heeren to be helpful. He is a science writer (a self-described "astrophysicist's interpreter and cosmic reporter") who has interviewed the leading brains of science (well, the *brains* were encapsulated in the craniums of the *people* he interviewed), such as Stephen Hawking, Nobel-prize winners, and leading NASA researchers. In his book *Show Me God,* Fred Heeren identifies several features of the First Big Cause that are logically evident from the nature of the universe:

1. *The First Big Cause must be independent of the universe itself.* Because things don't make themselves, the First Big Cause couldn't be a part of the universe. It has to exist outside of the universe. It not only has to be out of this world; it also has to be above and beyond all that is in the universe.

2. *The First Big Cause must be all-powerful.* Think about the power output and the quantity of material that exists within our universe. The First Big Cause that brought about all of that must be infinitely bigger than it all.

3. *The First Big Cause must be timeless.* Anything within our universe is trapped by the boundaries of time. Nothing in the universe could predate the beginning of our universe. Because the First Big Cause started the universe, then the First Big Cause is outside our time parameters. From our time perspective, the First Big Cause always existed and is without a beginning.

4. *The First Big Cause must be supernatural.* Just as the First Big Cause is outside our time parameters, it must also be outside the physical realm. It transcended the physical realm before the physical universe existed.

5. *The First Big Cause must be of supreme intelligence.* As we will discuss in chapters 5–9, the wonders of the universe (from the solar system to your pancreas) are tremendously complex. And whether we are talking about orbiting planets or your digestive system, they all work together with great symmetry and harmony. Scientists acknowledge this precision by referring to it as the "fine-tuning" within the universe. To put all of this incredible complexity into place, the First Big Cause must have the knowledge that encompasses and surpasses all of it. Here is what Albert Einstein had to say about the intelligence of the First Big Cause:

> The harmony of natural law...reveals an intelligence of such superiority that, compared with it, all the systematic thinking and acting of human beings is an utterly insignificant reflection.

6. *The First Big Cause must have a personality.* We aren't talking about a personality in the sense of being "perky" or "outgoing." We mean a personality in the sense that the First Big Cause must have acted intentionally—on purpose—with a particular result in mind. Heeren refers to this as "personhood." He cites prominent agnostic scientists who have written on the clearly evidenced purpose or intention they see behind intelligent life in this universe.

With these profile characteristics, you might think it would be easy to identify the First Big Cause. (You can immediately rule out everyone from your high school graduating class.) But wait! We can't look within our own universe and expect to find the First Big Cause (see Nos. 1 and 4 above). And peering outside the time-space continuum of our own universe is rather difficult. So how can we be expected to figure out this most important "who done it" question?

Remember how we said that the First Big Cause must have a personality? (If you don't, then review No. 6 above. It was only two paragraphs ago. So either slow down and stop speed-reading, or take a little gingko biloba for your memory.) Maybe that personality does include being "outgoing," since it seems that the First Big Cause wants to get "up close and personal" with you. It seems that the First Big Cause left a book that tells the whole story. You can probably find this book at the library. A much quicker way to find this book is to rent a motel room and look at the book in the nightstand. (This approach assumes that there is a Gideon Bible in the nightstand, because we aren't talking about the phone directory.)

The Bible Shows That God Fits the Profile of the First Big Cause

The Bible doesn't beat around a burning bush when it comes to identifying God as the First Big Cause. It says it in the very first verse:

> *In the beginning God created the heavens and the earth* (Genesis 1:1).

That's pretty clear. The Bible proclaims God as the Great Initiator. It says He was the First Big Cause that produced the effect of the universe.

But the Bible doesn't stop with just proclaiming God as the First Big Cause. It goes on throughout its pages to describe God's characteristics (referred to as *attributes* by theologians who don't want to use normal words like *characteristics*). These characteristics show that God perfectly fits the profile that scientists have determined would be required of the First Big Cause. Let's review the list, and this time we will insert the theologians' terminology for the particular God-attribute that fits the profile:

> 1. ***God is transcendent (independent of the universe itself).*** The Bible describes God as being separate from and independent of humanity, nature, and the universe. God is not simply connected to or involved with His creation; He is superior to it. This principle is explained in several significant ways.
>
> If God created the universe (Genesis 1:1), then He couldn't have been a part of it. He had to exist outside of

it. The Old Testament underscores this principle when it says that God existed before the mountains were created (Psalm 90:2). The New Testament repeats the theme by stating that He laid the foundations of the earth and will remain after the earth perishes (Hebrews 1:10-11).

His greatness, power, and knowledge reveal His transcendence (Isaiah 6:1-5).

It is also emphasized in the description of His holiness:

> *The high and lofty one who inhabits eternity, the Holy One, says this: "I live in that high and holy place"* (Isaiah 57:15).

Even God's thoughts transcend the best thinking of humanity:

> *"My thoughts are completely different from yours," says the LORD. "And my ways are far beyond anything you could imagine. For just as the heavens are higher than the earth, so are my ways higher than your ways and my thoughts higher than your thoughts" (Isaiah 55:8-9).*

You'll Have to Look Beyond the Universe to Find Him

The Russian cosmonaut Yuri Gagarin thought he had disproved the existence of God when he returned from orbiting the earth and said, "I didn't see any God out there!"

Yuri was evidently not aware of the First Big Cause profile No. 1. If God is greater than the universe, Yuri shouldn't have expected to see God trapped in the very thing He created.

2. God is omnipotent (all-powerful). There is no problem with God having the power to create the universe. He is defined as being the Source of all power. He is able to do all things (which includes creating the solar systems, but omits making 2+2=5).

A Hebrew name for God, *El-Shaddai,* described His unlimited power. Here is how the English translation reads:

The Lord appeared to him and said, "I am God Almighty" (Genesis 17:1).

God's omnipotence is often described in the Old Testament:

O Sovereign LORD! You have made the heavens and earth by your great power. Nothing is too hard for you! (Jeremiah 32:17).

In the New Testament, Jesus made similar statements about God the Father:

Jesus looked at them intently and said, "Humanly speaking, it is impossible. But with God everything is possible" (Matthew 19:26).

3. God is eternal (timeless). God is infinite in relationship to time. He was before time began. The dimension of time does not apply to Him.

He referred to Himself in terms that reveal His eternal nature:

"I am the Alpha and the Omega [the first and last letters of the Greek alphabet]—the beginning and the end," says the Lord God. "I am the one who is, who always was, and who is still to come, the Almighty One" (Revelation 1:8).

Other descriptions concur that He is timeless:

You are God, without beginning or end (Psalm 90:2).

4. God is a spirit (supernatural). God is Spirit. He is not composed of matter and does not possess a physical nature. Because He does not have a physical body, He is

How Old Is God Anyway?

If God existed before the universe began (let's round off and say roughly 10-15 billion years ago), you might be thinking that He is getting pretty old and crotchety by now. But you can't try to put an age on God. For Him, birthdays are inapplicable. Infinity plus one is no more than infinity. Or, infinity plus 15 billion years is no more than infinity. That's why the Bible describes Him as being "in the beginning, now, and forevermore" (Jude 25).

not limited to our dimensions of geographical location or space.

This principle was stated succinctly by Jesus:

God is Spirit (John 4:24).

God's supernatural spiritual nature is also implied in many verses that refer to His invisibility:

For at the right time Christ will be revealed from heaven by the blessed and only almighty God, the King of kings and Lord of lords. He alone can never die, and he lives in light so brilliant that no human can approach him. No one has ever seen him, nor ever will (1 Timothy 6:15-16).

5. *God is omniscient (supreme intelligence).* Knowledge of all things belongs to God. He alone knows the mighty principles that He engaged when He created the universe. He knows the laws of nature because He put them in place.

He knows every scientific truth—even those that we have not yet discovered (and that "we" doesn't mean just Bruce & Stan, but is the universal "we" that includes the smartest scientists):

Nothing in all creation can hide from him (Hebrews 4:13).

His unlimited knowledge applies to all creation in a general sense:

How great is our LORD! His power is absolute! His understanding is beyond comprehension! (Psalm 147:5).

And, in a very specific and personal sense, God knows all of your thoughts, words, and deeds (which can be either comforting or intimidating, depending on what you are thinking, saying, and doing):

O LORD, you have examined my heart and know everything about me (Psalm 139:1).

6. ***God is a being (personality).*** God is not some amorphous "force" (as in the *Star Wars* movies). He is personal. He is an individual being with self-consciousness. He has a will and is capable of feelings.

God indicated that He was not an abstract, unknowable being when He told Moses that He had a name:

God replied, "I Am the One Who Always Is....This will be my name forever; it has always been my name, and it will be used throughout all generations" (Exodus 3:14-15).

His personality is shown by His desire to stay connected with humanity:

Is the one who made your ears deaf? Is the one who formed your eyes blind?...He knows everything—doesn't he also know what you are doing? (Psalm 94:9-10).

The existence of His personality is best reflected by the Bible's explanation that God sacrificed His Son to provide the human race with a way to obtain eternal life with God Himself:

For God so loved the world that he gave his only Son, so that everyone who believes in him will not perish but have eternal life (John 3:16).

The God of the Bible fits the profile of the First Big Cause perfectly. And the Bible's descriptions of His character traits were not hastily scribbled down after computer data from the COBE satellite confirmed the big bang. The Bible was written centuries ago, and these character traits of God were cast in stone (or at least etched on papyrus and parchment) long before the scientists of the twentieth and twenty-first centuries developed a profile for the First Big Cause. From about 1500 B.C. (when Moses wrote Genesis), the Bible has been declaring that God created the universe. Now, about 3500 years later, the profile of the First Big Cause seems to confirm what the Bible has been saying all along.

---

*W*hat About the Gods of Other Religions?

In this chapter we are looking at the "God" alternative for the creation of the universe. (Chapter 3 is the "no God" alternative.) We don't have to analyze every single religion. We can limit discussion to those religions that present a God that fits the profile of the Big First Cause.

The religions that rely upon the Bible (which would include the Moslem, Jewish, and Christian religions) are the only ones that have a God that satisfies the criteria of the First Big Cause. Moses wrote the first five books of the Bible (including the book of Genesis, which details the sequence of how God created the universe and everything within it). Moses and the Hebrews (which is not a pop-singing group from the 1970s) were alone among all of the ancient peoples of the world in believing in a God who created the universe. The Hebrews believed in a monotheistic God that existed before the universe was created.

The gods of other religions don't have the First Big Cause characteristics. For example:

- Some religions believe in an eternal universe that gave birth to their god. The First Big Cause, however, must exist separate and independent from the universe.

- In most of the Eastern religions, there is no personal deity. In Hinduism, for example, reality is Brahma, and one does not relate to reality by turning outward to God, but instead by withdrawing inward through a process of contemplation. Nirvana is the stage at which all individual striving ceases and one becomes simply at rest within the universe.

- Many ancient religions had gods with restricted jurisdictional limits and powers. In a PBS television series called *Testament,* archaeologist John Romer stated that the God of the Hebrews was unique among all other gods because of His ability to move through both space and time, transcending them both.

And we have arbitrarily ruled out the religions that have historical errors, that make statements that can be scientifically proven to be false, or that describe the earth as being carried on the back of a giant sea turtle.

What Does the Bible Know About Science?

Scientists, philosophers, and theologians are pretty much agreed about this: It is the function of science to determine the facts of the universe; it is the function of religion to determine the meaning of the universe. If that is the case, then are we making a mistake by relying on the Bible for scientific information (such as the origin of the universe)?

God Uses Science and the Bible to Tell Us About Himself and the World

God could have chosen any method He wanted to tell us about Himself and to prove His existence. Remember, He has those omniscient and omnipotent characteristics going for Him, so He could do whatever He wanted. But God wants us to decide about Him for ourselves without forcing Himself on us (more about this in chapter 10). That ruled out options like arranging the planets to spell out "It's Me—God!" or waking the human race from its sleep each morning with a booming Darth Vader-type voice saying, "It's 6:15 A.M. Now get out of bed and worship Me!" God is more subtle than that.

God chose two methods to reveal facts about Himself and His involvement in our world.

How Can the Bible Be Scientifically Accurate If It Was Written by a Bunch of Shepherds and Fishermen?

Parts of the Bible were written by unschooled shepherds and fishermen, but other parts were written by highly educated men. (Moses attended the leading university in Egypt.) But the scientific credentials of these men don't matter, because God was really the Author of the Bible. The Bible says that these men were "inspired" by God to write the words (2 Peter 1:21). God used human agents to write down what He wanted to say.

Divine inspiration explains why the Bible is so scientifically accurate. Take, for example, the sequence of Creation events. Astrophysicist Hugh Ross has calculated that the odds of Moses correctly guessing all of the details of the origin and proper order for the development of Earth (and life on Earth) are less than one in trillions. Moses might have been a good guesser, but he couldn't have been that good. The only explanation for the scientific accuracy of the Bible is that God used His knowledge (there's that omniscience again) as the Bible's source of information.

Method One: General Revelation. God uses the world (nature) to disclose facts about Himself.

The heavens tell of the glory of God. The skies display his marvelous craftsmanship (Psalm 19:1).

From the time the world was created, people have seen the earth and sky and all that God made. They can clearly see his invisible qualities—his eternal power and divine nature. So they have no excuse whatsoever for not knowing God (Romans 1:20).

The disciplines of science can be used to make discoveries about the world (nature). These scientific findings can be interpreted to discover the truth about God.

Method Two: Special Revelation. God uses His Word (the Bible—Scripture) to disclose facts about Himself. Theology systematizes our study of the Scriptures. The Scriptures can be interpreted to discover the truth about God.

But what if the answers given by these methods contradict each other? If God gives us both His Word and science, is it possible for them to be in conflict? In cases of contradictory conclusions, which one should be believed and which one should be discredited?

These are good questions, but they assume that God can contradict Himself with inconsistencies between scientific fact and biblical revelation. But this cannot happen. One of the other personality traits of God is *truth.*

> *And he who is the Glory of Israel will not lie, nor will he change his mind* (1 Samuel 15:29).

> *So God has given us both his promise and his oath. These two things are unchangeable because it is impossible for God to lie* (Hebrews 6:18).

God speaks about things the way they really are. Whether He is talking about Himself or His creation, He speaks the truth. He cannot do otherwise.

While there can be no *real* contradictions between God's Word and science, we readily admit that there can be *apparent* discrepancies when science seems to say one thing and the Bible appears to say the opposite. How should that situation be handled?

Here are two guidelines you can use for handling what appear to be contradictions between science and the Bible:

> **1. Remember that the Bible is not a science textbook.** It was written for the primary purpose of revealing God's plan to establish a relationship with mankind. So it is more focused on who God is and who we are from a relational point of view. (That's why the Bible often uses

metaphors of a father or a shepherd to explain how God cares for us.) While the Bible contains some scientific information, it wasn't intended to explain all scientific intricacies and mathematical formulas. You don't expect *science* to describe the way a shepherd cares for his sheep, and you shouldn't expect the *Bible* to explain how to clone a sheep.

There are many matters that the Bible doesn't talk about (such as dinosaurs, cavemen, and male pattern baldness). The fact that the Bible is silent about these matters doesn't mean that it is wrong, or misinformed, or untrustworthy. It just means that God didn't feel compelled to talk about them.

2. *Remember that both methods by which God reveals Himself (the Bible and science) involve interpretation.* An apparent conflict might be due to an incorrect interpretation of facts of Scripture. The discrepancy may be cleared up in time.

---

*B*iblical "Errors" Proven Correct by Subsequent Scientific Discoveries

God has an unfair advantage over scientists. He has known everything since before time began. (There's that omniscience trait again.) Scientists have to learn facts the hard way—they have to discover them. Since some parts of the Bible were written almost 3500 years ago (and even the newest parts of the Bible were written almost 2000 years ago), many of its scientific statements were made before crucial scientific discoveries had been made. What might have appeared to be an erroneous statement in the Bible when it was made, has later proven to be correct when science finally got its act together. Here is a short list of examples prepared by astrophysicist Hugh Ross:

What the Bible Said:	What Scientists Once Thought:	What Science Now Knows:
The earth is a sphere— Isaiah 40:22.	The earth is flat.	The earth is a sphere.

There are more than one billion stars— Jeremiah 33:22.	There are only 1100 stars.	There are more than one billion stars.
Every star is different— 1 Corinthians 15:41.	All stars are the same.	Every star is different.
Light travels— Job 38:19-20.	Light is fixed in place.	Light travels.
Air has weight— Job 28:25.	Air is weightless.	Air has weight.
Winds blow in cyclones— Ecclesiastics 1:6.	Winds blow straight.	Winds blow in cyclones.
Blood is a source of life and healing— Leviticus 17:11.	Sick people must be bled (drained by a leech).	Blood is a source of life and healing.

The Biblical Account of the Days of Creation

As we said at the beginning of this chapter, there are only two alternatives to the beginning of the universe: Either God was involved, or He wasn't. God or no God. Since this chapter is devoted to the "God" alternative, it seems appropriate that we conclude by reviewing what the Bible says about how God created the universe (and all that is within it). This is known as the "Creation story." But don't think *story* is being used in the sense of a fable, legend, or fairy tale. The Bible presents this account as a true, real-life, and factual event.

Our review of the Bible's account of Creation is more than just a mental stroll through the Garden of Eden. We haven't forgotten our promise to be objective and analytical about all of this. So after we review what the Bible says about the origins of our universe, then we'll see if that explanation is consistent with modern scientific findings.

The Bible doesn't waste any time getting to the Creation story. It starts at the very first verse (which is a natural place for a beginning to start). As you probably know, the Creation sequence is described in a series of six "days."

Day 1: God Gets a Big Bang out of Creation

God existed, but the universe did not. Then, at God's command, the universe came into existence, complete with planet Earth with its own "solar system" (the sun by day and the moon by night).

> *In the beginning God created the heavens and the earth. The earth was empty, a formless mass cloaked in darkness. And the Spirit of God was hovering over its surface. Then God said, "Let there be light," and there was light. And God saw that it was good. Then he separated the light from the darkness. God called the light "day" and the darkness "night." Together these made up one day* (Genesis 1:1-5).

Okay, the universe is in place. But the Bible wasn't designed to be a cosmology textbook, so after Day 1 the perspective shifts from what is happening in outer space to the earth itself. Remember, the Bible is interested in explaining the relationship between God and people, so Moses wasn't going to waste words discussing the Andromeda galaxy or whether there was plant life on Uranus. (We hear that snickering.)

Day 2: Water Evaporates into Thin Air

The next thing God did was to get the water cycle going. Day 1 left the earth with a murky atmosphere, but the combination of sunlight and evaporation put clouds in the sky. On a grand scale, the evaporation caused the water on the surface of the earth to recede as rain clouds formed.

> *And God said, "Let there be space between the waters, to separate water from water." And so it was. God made this space to separate the waters above from the waters below. And God called the space "sky." This happened on the second day* (Genesis 1:6-8).

Day 3: Earth Becomes a Seedy Place

As the water on Earth receded in Day 2, the ground was revealed. With the cloudy atmosphere and all that evaporation, the earth had a giant greenhouse effect. Since God knew all about botany (remember that omniscience characteristic), He knew this would be a perfect growing climate for plants. So He created them.

> *And God said, "Let the waters beneath the sky be gathered into one place so dry ground may appear." And so it was. God named the dry ground "land" and the water "seas." And God saw that it was good. Then God said, "Let the land burst forth with every sort of grass and seed-bearing plant. And let there be trees that grow seed-bearing fruit. The seeds will then produce the kinds of plants and trees from which they came." And so it was. The land was filled with seed-bearing plants and trees, and their seeds produced plants and trees of like kind. And God saw that it was good. This all happened on the third day* (Genesis 1:9-13).

What a Difference a Day Makes

The Bible's Book of Genesis was written in the Hebrew language. The word *day* in Hebrew has several different meanings. It can be used to mean a workday (like eight hours), or a full day (as in 24 hours), or a long period of time (as in thousands of years). The proper interpretation of the six "days" in the Genesis Creation account has been the subject of considerable debate. We devote all of chapter 4 to discussing this topic. For now, let's just focus on the sequence of the "days" and not get hung up on the duration.

Day 4: On a Clear Day, You Can See Forever

The plants started growing, and you know what that means...photosynthesis (or have you forgotten that display board you made for your fifth grade science fair?). The production of oxygen from the plants cleared up the atmosphere. The sky changed from murky to transparent (kind of like an atmospheric Clearasil). For the first time the sun, moon, and stars became clearly visible.

> And God said, "Let bright lights appear in the sky to separate the day from the night. They will be signs to mark off the seasons, the days, and the years. Let their light shine down upon the earth." And so it was. For God made two great lights, the sun and the moon, to shine down upon the earth. The greater one, the sun, presides during the day; the lesser one, the moon, presides through the night. He also made the stars. God set these lights in the heavens to light the earth, to govern the day and the night, and to separate the light from the darkness. And God saw that it was good. This all happened on the fourth day (Genesis 1:14-19).

God didn't *create* the sun, moon, and stars on Day 4. (That had already happened in Day 1.) But the atmosphere cleared up in Day 4 so that they became apparent for the first time from the perspective of an observer on Earth.

Day 5: Fish Gotta Swim and Birds Gotta Fly

With all of those oceans and all of that clear sky, God created things to go in them:

> And God said, "Let the waters swarm with fish and other life. Let the skies be filled with birds of every kind." So God created great sea creatures and every sort of fish and every kind of bird. And God saw that it was good. Then God blessed them, saying, "Let the fish multiply and fill the oceans. Let the birds increase and fill the earth." This all happened on the fifth day (Genesis 1:20-23).

Day 6: Lions and Tigers and Adam and Eve

Let's see, we've got vegetables (Day 3) and fish and poultry (Day 5). But God knew that you can't have a really successful restaurant unless you've got beef on the menu.

> And God said, "Let the earth bring forth every kind of animal—livestock, small animals, and wildlife." And so it was. God made all sorts of wild animals, livestock, and small animals, each able to reproduce more of its own kind. And God saw that it was good (Genesis 1:24-25).

We're getting toward the end of Day 6, and one thing is still missing. Have you noticed what it is? You! (Well, not you exactly, but your ancestors.) Fortunately for you (and us), God had a little more work to accomplish on Day 6:

> Then God said, "Let us make people in our image, to be like ourselves. They will be masters over all life—the fish in the sea, the birds in the sky, and all the livestock, wild animals, and small animals." So God created people in his own image; God patterned them after himself; male and female he created them....Then God looked over all he had made, and he saw that it was excellent in every way. This all happened on the sixth day (Genesis 1:26-27,31).

Wow! That was a good week's work. Aren't you glad God did all of this before labor laws and unions enforced a five-day work-week?

The Bible's Sequence Is in Sync with Science

If God is all-knowing, then He knew about science before the invention of the lab coat. So we know He wasn't losing sleep worrying about whether the Bible's Creation account would be supported by scientific findings. But just in case *you* are wondering about this, the biblical sequence of Creation events matches precisely with scientific findings for the sequence of the origins of the universe, the formation of Earth, and the beginnings of life.

Check out the symmetry of the sequences for yourself:

Day	Biblical Sequence	Scientific Sequence
1	Heavens and Earth are created	The big bang
2	The waters separate	Earth's atmosphere changes
3	Dry land appears; plant life begins	Bacteria and algae grow
4	Sun, moon, and stars are visible	Earth's atmosphere becomes transparent
5	First animal life in water and air	Multicellular life appears in water; winged insects appear
6	Land animals and humans appear	Land animals appear; later human life appears

We aren't trying to cram this "God alternative" down your throat. We totally respect your right to decide for yourself what you believe about the origins of the universe. But we do hope you can see that the "God alternative" isn't totally unreasonable, as some people would want you to believe. In fact, we think you'll find it entirely reasonable and consistent with science.

"What's That Again?"

1. There are certain logical and rational characteristics that must be attributed to the First Big Cause that produced the beginning of the universe. It must be independent from the universe, all-powerful, timeless, supernatural, of supreme intelligence, and possess a personality (to be intentional and purposeful).

2. Centuries before philosophers and scientists determined the characteristics of the First Big Cause,
   the Bible declared that God had all of these traits.

3. Only the God of the Bible fits the profile of the
   First Big Cause. The gods of other religions don't fit
   the profile.

4. Not only does God meet the criteria of the First Big
   Cause, but the Bible also states that God created the
   universe and everything within it.

5. The sequence of the biblical account of Creation
   matches exactly with the scientific timetable for
   the formation of the universe and all life-forms on
   Earth.

6. The possibility that God created the univere is a
   reasonable alternative that merits your consideration.

Dig Deeper

If you are interested in an overview on who God is, allow us to shamelessly recommend our book *Bruce & Stan's Guide to God*. It includes a great discussion of the characteristics of God (if we do say so ourselves).

If you want to know how science matches up with the biblical account of Creation, then you've got to read *The Creator and the Cosmos* by Hugh Ross, Ph.D. This author is a genius, but he does a great job of explaining how recent scientific discoveries point to God.

If you are looking for a good discussion on logical reasons for belief in God, then you might enjoy *Faith & Reason: Searching for a Rational Faith* by Ronald H. Nash.

If you are intrigued by astronomy, we are sure you will find *Show Me God* by Fred Heeren to be fascinating. It is filled with compelling arguments and Heeren's interviews with some of the world's top cosmologists, including Stephen Hawking.

■ ■ ■

*Q*uestions for *R*eflection and *D*iscussion

1. Explain what the phrase *ex nihilo nihil fit* means. Explain what it means in the context of the origin of the universe. Does God have any relation to this?

2. If there was a First Big Cause that brought about the effect of the creation of the universe, what are some things that must be true about the First Big Cause? In other words, based on what you know about the universe, what does this tell you about the traits of the First Big Cause?

3. Name as many attributes (characteristics) of God as you can think of. Explain how each attribute might fit the profile of the First Big Cause.

4. Can you think of a god or supreme being from any religion, other than the God of the Bible, that fits the profile of the First Big Cause? If the God of the Bible is the only one, is there anything significant about that?

5. Can you think of any holy book, other than the Bible, that has an explanation of the origin of the universe that matches the sequence as determined by science?

6. If you are looking for a religion to believe in, should it matter to you whether a religious faith has a credible account for how the world came into existence?

7. Read the Creation sequence in Genesis 1:1-31. Do you agree that the perspective of Day 1 seems to be from outer space looking down, while the perspective of Days 2-6 seems to be from Earth looking up and around? Why do you suppose the sequence is written this way?

8. As many times as you can, use the word "day" in a sentence to convey a different meaning or time period.

Moving On...

Suppose we told you that one side of the "God Versus No God" debate was narrow-minded and intolerant of the opposing viewpoint. Suppose we said that side was relying on outdated concepts and refused to acknowledge recent scientific findings. Suppose that we suggested the religious fervor of that group had overtaken rational thinking in an attempt to gain converts and capture adherents to its position. You might think that we were talking about the proponents of the "God" alternative.

Well, you would be wrong. It is the "no God" folks who seem to be promoting a religion—but it is a religion of no God.

Let's shift gears now and look at that other alternative: the one that believes there is no God involved in the beginning of the universe. It is a legitimate alternative and deserves to be analyzed. We think you'll be surprised, as we were, to learn that it is surrounded by a lot of weak logic and scientific *theories* that are promoted as *facts*.

We need to fairly and objectively consider the logical conclusions of the "no God" alternative (without getting caught up in the hype) so we can accurately frame the debate. You've got to fully understand the opposing sides of the issue before you'll be ready to weigh the scientific evidence from the chapters in Part Two.

So set the Bible aside and take off your halo. It's time to enter a universe with no God.

Chapter 3

It is absolutely safe to say that if you meet somebody who claims not to believe in evolution, that person is ignorant, stupid, or insane (or wicked, but I'd rather not consider that).

—Oxford scientist and author Richard Dawkins

In chapter 2, we reviewed the Bible's version of how everything began. But maybe you are skeptical about whether the Bible is scientifically accurate on that subject. Or, possibly you just don't believe any part of it. Or, maybe *you* believe it, but you have a hard time convincing other people that the Bible is believable—especially when it comes to the subject of how the universe and life began.

We think it is entirely legitimate to wonder whether God was really responsible for creating everything. The Bible says so, but is there any corroborating evidence? That is an honest question that deserves an honest investigation. Unfortunately, this question doesn't get an honest evaluation because the scientific establishment refuses to accept the possibility that God created the universe and life. The question never gets answered because we're not allowed to ask it.

If you like stories that involve an underdog fighting against an overbearing institution, then this chapter is for you. We'll tell you about a group of renegade scientists (with impeccable credentials) who are battling the establishment in an attempt to analyze scientific information to see whether it supports "God" or "no God." They've got answers to the questions that you aren't supposed to be asking. Aren't you curious?

What If God Doesn't Exist?

*S*uppose that you asked us to meet you at Starbucks to discuss how the world began. And suppose that our discussion brings us to opposing viewpoints.

You say: "I don't think God had anything to do with the beginning of the universe or life. I don't even think God exists."

After scooting our chairs away from you just in case you are suddenly struck by a bolt of lightning, we say: "We believe that God was the First Big Cause that began the universe and that He was actively involved in starting all forms of life on Earth." (And if you wanted a more detailed explanation, we would tell you to reread chapter 2.)

Now, the three of us are rational adults (with momentary exceptions), so we wouldn't get into a shouting match with each other. We're pretty sure that we could discuss this subject with you calmly and sensibly, without the animosity that might otherwise qualify us for an episode of the Jerry Springer Show. (This afternoon on Jerry: "Skeptics Who Slander Bruce & Stan," followed by high-lights of "I Married an Extraterrestrial Elvis Impersonator.")

Here's our point: A discussion of whether or not God was responsible for the beginnings of life doesn't have to be hostile. You would present your arguments for no God being involved, and we would tell you our reasons for believing that God was involved. The question of God's existence would get discussed from both per-spectives.

Unfortunately, civilization hasn't always been this open-minded:

- For many centuries, the predominant view in Western culture was that God created the earth and all of the life on it. Big-time religion pretty much squelched anyone from asking, "What if God doesn't exist?"

- Then about 150 years ago, the scientific community began to challenge that presumption of God and Cre-ation. In a very short period of time, God was removed from the picture. By now, He has been pushed so far out that the scientific establishment will not even tolerate the question, "What if God exists?"

What happened? How did things go from "God" to "no God" so quickly? Why can't the notion of God even be raised as a legit-imate scientific explanation for the origin of life?

Darwin and His Disciples

Back in 1859, a relatively obscure scientist by the name of Charles Darwin became fascinated with his observations from selective breeding experiments. From these observations, he developed a most interesting hypothesis of natural selection. This hypothesis formed the basis of his book *On the Origin of Species.* Here are the basic points:

- ***Random mutation:*** All plants and animals—any organism that exists—are the product of the random interplay of the known processes of heredity.

- ***Natural selection:*** Differential reproduction in organisms occurs as weak traits give way to stronger ones (survival of the fittest).

This was pretty controversial stuff, but the real shocker came in Darwin's subsequent book *The Descent of Man,* when he promoted the theory of *common descent:* All living creatures are descended from a single ancestor.

Here is what Darwin was saying in his theories:

- Life started on its own as a tiny cell that developed over time into all forms of life, including humans.

- Nature acted like a breeding machine and produced biological changes. As useful new traits appeared, they were passed on to the next generation. Harmful traits (or those of little use) were eliminated by Darwin's mechanism of natural selection.

- While these changes were small, over time and generations they accumulated until organisms developed new limbs, or organs, or other body parts. Given enough time, the organisms changed so much that they didn't resemble their ancestors anymore.

Darwin couldn't prove this theory because he didn't have the fossil evidence to back it up. But he acknowledged this fact:

The number of intermediate varieties, which have formerly existed on the earth, [must] be truly enormous. Why then is not every geological formation and every stratus full of such intermediate links? Geology assuredly does not reveal any such finely graded organic chain; and this, perhaps, is the most obvious and gravest objection which can be urged against my theory (from *On the Origin of Species)*.

Darwin wasn't worried about the lack of fossil evidence to back up this theory. He claimed that as the science and techniques of paleontology (fossil finding) progressed, the fossils would be found to prove his theory correct.

$\mathcal{T}$he "E" Word

While the "E" word was around before Darwin, it was his theory that made it controversial. Of course, we're talking about *evolution*. We'll be talking a lot about evolution in the rest of this book (and particularly in chapters 7 and 8). At this juncture, however, we think that it is important to take 60 seconds to get our terminology straight.

Here are a few important things you need to know about the term *evolution*:

1. Contrary to what you might have heard some preacher say, *evolution* is not a dirty word.

2. There are two basic types of evolution:

    Microevolution refers to minor variations at or below the species level. For example, studies in the Galapagos Islands show that the average size and thickness of finch beaks increased during a drought by five percent because the surviving birds had to have tougher beaks to crack the few remaining hard seeds. When the rains returned and seeds were again plentiful, beak sizes returned to normal. The fact that organisms vary and adapt to changing environmental conditions is not controversial. Microevolution is well supported by scientific evidence.

    Macroevolution refers to major innovations such as new organs (like eyes), structures (like wings), or body plans. The origin of birds and scientific observers in the first place would be examples of macroevolution. Whether gradual, undirected, microevolutionary changes accumulate from bacteria to create birds and scientists is highly controversial.

3. If people are talking about evolution, you have to determine which type they mean. If they say that "science proves evolution," that statement is true—if they are talking about microevolution; or false—if they are talking about macroevolution.

Okay, that's it. Your 60 seconds are about up. Now you can go back to the regular text. (If you are a speed-reader, you might even have enough time left over to make a run to the refrigerator for a quick snack.)

Darwinism was what some people were waiting for. Under his theory of macroevolution (aren't you glad that you read the box on the previous page?), Darwin was saying that people were not created by a purposeful being (God). Instead, people are just the product of a mindless, materialistic evolutionary process. As you might imagine, people who believed the Bible detested this hypothesis, but it was very popular with people who chose not to believe in God. For anyone who didn't want to believe the Bible, Darwin's theory gave an alternative explanation for how the human race came into existence.

In truth, from the period of the earliest stages of Greek thought man has been eager to discover some natural cause of evolution, and to abandon the idea of supernatural intervention in the order of nature.

—Henry Fairfield Osborn, head of the American Museum of Natural History and proponent of evolution (1925)

Darwinism isn't so much a scientific theory as it is a philosophy. And in a sense, it is more than just a philosophy to its adherents. To them it is a religion—a religion that explains the world in strictly naturalistic terms without a God. *Time* magazine recognized this when it wrote: "Charles Darwin didn't want to murder God, as he once put it. But he did."

The whole point of Darwinism is to explain the world in a way that excludes any role for a Creator. What is being sold in the name of science is a completely naturalistic understanding of reality.

—Phillip Johnson

Teaching It Doesn't Make It True: Detecting Defects in Darwinism

Darwin's theory has survived and flourished since he proclaimed it in 1859. It is taught as a fundamental precept of biological science without any disclaimer or mention of anomalies or ambiguities. So it must be correct, right? Wrong.

Darwinism is *not* so obviously true that it should be accepted as fact instead of theory. Although Darwin's theory has had almost 150 years to be proven by scientific findings, significant problems remain:

- *Fossil evidence.* Most fossils of new species appear all at once, fully formed, and change very little throughout their existence. In other words, the major pattern in the fossil record does not show gradual changes and variations from one species moving into another. There are few, if any, undisputed intermediary stages. We'll talk more about this in chapter 7, but just so you know that evolution is not a scientific slam dunk, look at what noted paleontologist Niles Eldredge said about lingering suspicions of Darwin's mechanism of change:

  > If it is true that an influx of doubt and uncertainty actually marks periods of healthy growth in science, then evolutionary biology is flourishing today as it seldom has in the past. For biologists are collectively less agreed upon the details of evolutionary mechanics than they were a scant decade ago. Moreover, many scientists have advocated fundamental revisions of orthodox evolutionary theory.

- *Irreducible complexity.* Darwin's theory won't work if there is a complex organ that couldn't have been formed in progressive, gradual stages. This is the principle of "irreducible complexity," which states that some organisms are comprised of basic component parts, and the organism wouldn't exist (because it couldn't function) without all of the component parts existing at the same time. Darwin himself admitted that his theory would fail if it could be shown that irreducible complexity existed in nature:

> If it could be demonstrated that any complex organ existed which could not possibly have been formed by numerous, successive, slight modifications, my theory would absolutely break down (from *On the Origin of Species*).

At the time Darwin made this statement, biologists basically considered the cell to be little more than a blob. They simply didn't have the technology to examine it closely. Contemporary science, however, has found that many systems in living organisms are irreducibly complex. The complexity in these organisms is too extreme for Darwinism to be plausible. They consist of several parts, all of which must be present for the system to work. Here is what the internationally renowned biochemist Michael Behe has said about this flaw in Darwin's theory:

> To Darwin, the cell was a "black box"—its inner workings were utterly mysterious to him. Now, the black box has been opened up and we know how it works. Applying Darwin's test to the ultra-complex world of molecular machinery and cellular systems that have been discovered over the past 40 years, we can say that Darwin's theory has "absolutely broken down."

We'll talk more about irreducible complexity in chapter 10, but for now we'll change the subject. We don't want your brain to overheat!

Science, Schmience! What's the Big Deal?

Some supporters of Darwinism readily admit that their theories are based as much on philosophical assumptions as on scientific evidence. The scientific establishment holds onto prejudices that favor Darwin (despite shaky and scanty evidence) and rejects any notion of God. So why don't we just let science retain its prejudices, and the discussions of God can be left to the disciplines of theology and philosophy?

In our culture, science is considered the only valid test for knowledge and truth. If it is "science," then we believe it. Particularly within our Western society, neither philosophy, nor religion, nor literature, nor law, nor music, nor art can make any such cognitive claim. (This is especially true of religion, which is considered to have no universal truth that is applicable to all peoples.) For most of us, these other disciplines are rejected as sources of truth in favor of science. Many see this as just a matter of intellectual honesty:

- Philosophy is just a bunch of people sitting around thinking lofty thoughts.

- Theology is just a matter of faith—you can believe whatever you are willing to put your faith in.

- Art is the appreciation of colors and shapes, but no tangible benefit comes from it.

- The law is just a bunch of rules that are so complicated and arbitrarily enforced that they actually encourage disobedience (talk about irreducible complexity).

But science, oh sweet science. It is the elixir that we seek to quench our intellectual thirst. (Sorry, we got carried away.) What we mean is that science leads our culture and stands at the forefront of intellectual integrity. It has given us technology that has improved our lives. It has found cures for our diseases. It informs us about our past and gives us the ability to look into the depths of outer space. And the findings and benefits of science are universally applicable to peoples of all countries, ethnicities, and faiths. Science seems to be the only universal constant in our lives upon which we can rely.

So if we want to have a straightforward, legitimate discussion with you about whether God was involved in creating the world and life (remember our little meeting at Starbucks that began this chapter?), then we have to bring it into the realm of science. To leave a discussion about God out of the scientific arena is to fail to ask important questions and opt out of the great origins debate. Since Darwinism is a pervasive tenet of the scientific establishment, the subject of the possibility of God's involvement in the origins of the universe must be discussed at the scientific level.

Darwinism is in direct conflict with the Bible because the Bible teaches that:

- Nature is not self-sufficient (Colossians 1:16-17).

- God created nature as well as the laws by which nature operates (Genesis 1).

- God specially and specifically created life (Genesis 1).

- God upholds the world moment by moment (Romans 11:36).

If Darwinism is wrong and the Bible is right, then we will only discover that fact if we are allowed to discuss the evidence of God's involvement in Creation at the scientific level.

Signs of Intelligent Design

Arguments for God's involvement in nature have been around for centuries, but these arguments were always in the realm of theology and philosophy. As far back as the fourth century, guys like Minuchius Felix reasoned that nature exhibits features that nature itself cannot explain, which require an intelligence beyond nature. Arguments for "intelligent design" were continued by the likes of Thomas Aquinas in the thirteenth century. These arguments seemed to be quite persuasive at the time. (That was back in the days when philosophy and theology were more respected than science—back in the days when science was suggesting leeches as a preferred medical technique.)

The "Designer" Watch

One of the most famous intelligent-design arguments belongs to William Paley from his work *Natural Theology,* published in 1802. Paley introduced the analogy of the watchmaker.

In Paley's analogy, you are walking through a field and find a watch. The watch has a function (telling time). You could be sure that the watch was a result of intelligence (there was a watchmaker) and not the result of undirected natural processes. In other words, the watch—with all its intricate, delicate parts—didn't just fall into place by itself.

Paley saw the watch as an analogy to the eye in a mammal. The eye obviously has a specific function, and it must be the result of an intelligent designer because the parts are too intricate to have just fallen into place by themselves.

Philosophical and theological arguments for intelligent design were fine back in the days of leeches, but what about now, when science is the final arbiter of truth? Now that lofty thoughts and faith aren't in vogue, we have to look for hard evidence. But is there any? Can intelligent design be proven by observation or experiment? Philosophizing and faith are one thing (actually, they are two things), but empirical evidence is something else. For empirical evidence we need to go to science.

Within the last decade or so, a group of top-notch scientists from different specialties have burst into the science lab to promote scientific research referred to as "intelligent design." All of a sudden, the arguments for intelligent design have come out of the theology/philosophy closet and are bubbling like a test tube held over a Bunsen burner. (Please pardon the mix of metaphors.)

For about the last 150 years, the theory of intelligent design was kept out of the scientific mainstream because there were no precise methods for distinguishing intelligently caused objects from unintelligently caused ones. But now...

- Scientists are beginning to realize that intelligent design can be formulated as a scientific theory.

- Improved technology and new scientific techniques and methods now allow scientists to distinguish between intelligently caused objects and unintelligently caused ones.

In biology, for example, intelligent design is a theory of biological origins and development. Its fundamental claim is that intelligent causes are necessary to explain the complex, information-rich structures of biology and that these causes are empirically detectable. There exist well-defined methods that, on the basis of observational features of the world, are capable of reliably distinguishing intelligent cause from undirected natural causes.

Intelligent design approaches science from the opposite perspective of Darwinism. Darwinism is all about undirected natural causes instead of intelligent causes. Intelligent design is about finding that intelligent causes can do things that undirected natural causes cannot. Since we work with letters better than formulas, let us give you an example of Darwinism and intelligent design using Scrabble letters.

Darwinism: If undirected natural causes were sprinkling Scrabble letters on a table, you would expect to find a random arrangement like this:

uTtf heSaea ebr oeoo hto khse arv aB rpurrcl enb aaenldic

Intelligent design: There would be evidence of intelligent design if you found those very same Scrabble letters sprinkled on the table in the following order:

**There are other Bruce & Stan books
available for purchase**

One of the leading scientific scholars involved with intelligent design is Dr. William Dembski. Here is how he describes the role of intelligent design:

> From observable features of the natural world, intelligent design infers an intelligence responsible for those features. The world contains events, objects and structures that exhaust the explanatory resources of undirected natural causes and that can be adequately explained only by recourse to intelligent causes.

It is important to note that the scientists supporting intelligent design do not oppose Darwinism because it contradicts the Bible or challenges sacred notions of Christianity. For these scientists, it is not about religion (some of them, in fact, describe themselves as agnostics).

The intelligent-design scientists do not think that Darwin was totally out to lunch. They acknowledge that Darwin's mutation-selection mechanism constitutes a respectable concept in biology that merits continued investigation. But Darwinism is much more than just the random mutation-natural selection mechanism. Darwinism is the all-encompassing claim that this undirected mechanism accounts for all the diversity of life and the common descent of all life-forms. The intelligent-design movement contends that the evidence does not support this broad claim. In their examination, intelligent-design scientists find that:

- The evidence only supports limited variation within fixed boundaries (this is the microevolution that we were talking about).

- But the random ability of organisms to diversify across all boundaries (macroevolution)—even if it is true—cannot be attributed solely to the mutation-selection mechanism.

For the intelligent-design movement, the following problems have proven to be fatal for Darwin's mutation-selection theory because they show that an undirected natural process cannot sufficiently answer questions about:

- the origin of life
- the origin of the information-rich genetic code
- the origin of multicellular life
- the origin of sexuality
- the absence of transitional forms in the fossil record
- the biological big bang of the Cambrian era (don't worry about this yet—wait until chapter 7)
- the development of complex organ systems
- the development of irreducibly complex molecular "machines"

*I*ntelligent Design Is Not...

Intelligent design does not speculate or theorize about the nature, character, or purposes of the intelligence that created the design. Intelligent design leaves to theology the task of figuring out who the intelligence is (whether the God of the Bible, some other god, or some other type of intelligence, for that matter). Intelligent design examines the evidence for design and from this evidence infers a designer. It doesn't try to figure out the designer's purpose or who the designer is.

This is similar to what happens when archaeologists find a tool crafted by some unknown tribe. They can easily identify that intelligence was involved without knowing the purpose for which the tool was made. They may speculate that the tool was designed as a weapon (when it was actually used for removing excess earwax). The fact that the *purpose* is unknown doesn't detract from the determination that *intelligence* was responsible for the object.

Hostile Territory: Bringing Intelligent Design to Darwin's World

Most Darwinists aren't very friendly toward the upstart intelligent designers. In fact, some of the reaction has been a little hostile. (There haven't been any brawls or street fights. Remember, these are scientists and brainy types. About the worst they could do is throw their pocket protectors at each other.)

Although he isn't a scientist, Phillip Johnson is one of the leaders of the intelligent design movement. He specializes in analyzing the attacks and arguments of the Darwinists. Phillip Johnson knows a lot about debate, logic, and making arguments. He ought to. He was a law clerk for the chief justice of the United States Supreme Court and has been a law professor at the University of California at Berkeley for more than 30 years. Johnson contends that the Darwinian establishment, in order to maintain its political, cultural, and intellectual authority, consistently engages in a *fallacy of equivocation*. This is the technique of using a term with multiple meanings:

- In defense of Darwinism, Michael Ruse wrote, "Evolution Is Fact, Fact, Fact!" But how is he using the term? Is it a fact that organisms have experienced limited change over time? Or is it a fact that the full diversity of life has evolved through purposeless naturalistic processes? The first use—microevolution—finds universal scientific agreement; the latter use—macroevolution—is open to debate.

- When they are on the attack, the Darwinists refer to the supporters of intelligent design as "creationists." This term is correct in the sense that intelligent design provides evidence from which one can infer a designer or a "creator." But that is not the sense in which the Darwinists use it. They refer to creationists as people who believe that the earth is only 6000 to 10,000 years old (often called "young earth creationists"—we'll talk about that in the next chapter). But this doesn't logically follow. Rejecting fully naturalistic macroevolution does not require acceptance of young earth Creation. In fact, many of the intelligent design scientists support the "old earth" theory, which puts the age of the earth at billions of years. But the Darwinists can create some suspicions about the intelligent design movement by calling them "creationists" because that term has multiple meanings.

Sticks and Stones

One of the "diversionary tactics" that Phillip Johnson has encountered from the Darwinists is the famous *ad hominem* (well, it must be famous to people who debate a lot because to us it just sounds like an infectious skin disease). This is the art of diverting attention away from the issue by attacking your opponent's character, personality, or qualifications. This is the technique employed by the Darwinists when:

- They avoid the scientific challenges to Darwinism by calling Phillip Johnson a "know-nothing lawyer" who doesn't understand "how science works."

- Darwinist Richard Dawkins dodges debate about evolution by calling anyone who supports intelligent design "ignorant, stupid, insane, or wicked" (see the quote on the title page for this chapter).

Intelligent Design Doesn't Stifle Scientific Investigation

Darwinists are quick to claim that intelligent design halts extensive scientific investigation: "The Intelligent Designer did it, so we don't have to search any further." But the Darwinists are wrong. The answers don't stop when it is determined that an object was intelligently designed. The issue of how it works is still a fruitful area for investigation.

William Dembski uses the illustration of a Stradivarius violin in explaining how intelligent design actually fosters in-depth scientific investigation. We know that a Stradivarius violin was designed. It didn't just emerge out of nothingness. We even know who designed it (duh, that would be Stradivarius). But we don't know *how* he did it. No one today can manufacture a violin as good as a Stradivarius. Since we know it was designed, we can apply "reverse engineering" to figure out how it was designed. Reverse engineering (figuring out how something designed could have been produced) requires learning as much as possible about it. There wouldn't be any "reverse engineering" if it was assumed to have fallen together by random and happenstance circumstances. Therefore, the criticism that intelligent design stifles scientific inquiry is unjustified.

> *Intelligent design is one intelligence determining what another intelligence has done.*
>
> —William A. Dembski

Searching for Design Is Not an Unscientific Activity

The Darwinists also like to attack intelligent design on the basis that *looking for design is unscientific.* The Darwinists are way out on the limb of the evolutionary tree with this misplaced argument. Science recognizes the search for intelligent design in many fields.

- Many industries depend on being able to distinguish accident from design: insurance fraud investigation, criminal justice, cryptography, patent and copyright protection. No one calls these industries "unscientific" simply because they look for evidence of design.

- Some scientific disciplines such as anthropology and archaeology could not exist without the detection of intelligent design. (How can the archaeologist say that the bowl-shaped object is "a bowl" unless it is assumed that an intelligence from a past society created it?)

- NASA's $100-million SETI project (Search for Extra-Terrestrial Intelligence) searched for intelligence in outer space. Your tax dollars paid for the world's largest satellite dish in an attempt to pick up any communication from intelligent life-forms in the cosmos. If looking for evidence of intelligence is not scientific, as the Darwinists claim, then why did NASA spend $100-million searching for it?

Investigating a scenario that appears to have been produced by something other than mere chance cannot be called "unscientific." Suppose a store manager bought a winning lottery ticket at his own store. Then suppose the next week his wife won on a ticket from his store. Then suppose his son won the following week. Under these circumstances, wouldn't you suspect that something more than chance was involved? You couldn't ignore the possibility of an outside influence. Such a situation certainly merits investigation to see if some outside "design" was involved (cheating, for example!). This kind of research is what intelligent design is all about.

Dealing with the Unobservable Doesn't Make Intelligent Design Unscientific

We think the Darwinists are getting a little desperate when they argue that intelligent design is unscientific because it appeals to unobservable objects or events. They are referring, of course, to the unobservable "designer." But intelligent design does not fail to be scientific just because the designer cannot easily be located.

Perhaps the Darwinists have forgotten that the whole theory of macroevolution revolves around the as yet unobservable "transitional life-forms." The major transitional life-forms that occupy the branching points on Darwin's tree of life have never been observed in the fossil record. They've been postulated only because they help Darwinists explain the variety of life-forms which are currently present, but all the postulating hasn't made them observable.

Intelligent Design Isn't Outside the Scope of Science

Darwinists contend that intelligent design doesn't belong in the scientific sphere because it is a theory more suited to theology. The Darwinists believe that intelligent design is contrary to science because its theory contradicts the random, undirected processes which are the essence of science. But that argument is based on the Darwinists' own narrow definition of science. The intelligent design movement puts forth a broader definition of science that follows the evidence (wherever it leads) for design and purpose.

According to the Darwinian establishment, evolution addresses a scientific question, whereas intelligent design addresses a religious question. (It is on this basis that Darwinism is taught in the schools, but intelligent design—although it promotes no "religion"—is prohibited from classroom instruction on the fallacious argument that it constitutes the establishment of religion by the State, which is prohibited by the Constitution.) The Darwinists view Darwinism and intelligent design to be mutually exclusive (which they are), but consider evolution as the only viable scientific option. Intelligent design does not even get a hearing.

- Science, according to the Darwinian establishment, excludes by definition everything except the undirected, random processes of nature.

- It follows then that all talk of purpose, design, and intelligence is barred from the discussion.

- By defining science as a form of inquiry restricted solely to what can be explained in terms of undirected natural processes, the Darwinian establishment has ruled intelligent design to be outside of science.

But intelligent design, on the other hand, views science as broad enough to seek an explanation that, in addition to undirected natural causes, may involve intelligent input and direction.

There is no danger that science will get sidetracked with arguments about religion from the intelligent design scientists. Darwinists are the ones who actually raise the issue of religion in the debates with intelligent design supporters. But the scientists representing intelligent design refuse to get diverted by questions like:

- Do you really believe that the whole universe was created in six 24-hour days?

- Could Jesus really have been God?

- If there is a God, why does He allow evil?

Intelligent design tries to keep everything on a scientific level. There is no talk about the character and nature of the designer.

Intelligent design is therefore not the study of intelligent causes per se but of information pathways induced by intelligent causes. As a result intelligent design presupposes neither a creator nor miracles. Intelligent design is theologically minimalist. It detects intelligence without speculating about the nature of the intelligence.

—William A. Dembski

Can We Finally Ask the Question?

Well, we have come a long way from our meeting at Starbucks at the beginning of this chapter. It started out innocently enough with a discussion about whether there was evidence to determine if the origin of the world involved "God" or "no God." So we've still got a question to deal with: What does the evidence in nature show: God or no God?

If we limit our scientific investigations to a framework of undirected natural causes, then science will necessarily be incapable of investigating God's interaction with the world. But if we permit science to investigate intelligent causes, then God's interaction with the world becomes a legitimate domain for scientific investigation.

Now that you are well-versed in the theories of Darwinism and intelligent design, we can ask our simple question in scientific terminology: Does the scientific evidence show that life originated from undirected, random processes, or does the evidence indicate that intelligent design was involved? That is the question that we will be asking in Part Two (chapters 5-10). We will be examining the evidence from the perspectives of Darwinism and intelligent design. So before we start staring into space, probing beneath the earth's crust, and sniffing out dinosaur fossils, let's review some crucial terminology.

Bruce & Stan's Lexicon—The Terminology That Frames the Debate

You already know that some terms used in the debate between Darwinism and intelligent design have multiple meanings. Things can get further confused because some concepts can be described by several different terms. Here is a short list of terminology that will be helpful to remember as we start analyzing the evidence in Part Two:

Common descent: The theory that all organisms have been linked in the past by common ancestors. This is a key component of Darwinism.

Creation: The meaning depends upon the context. In its simplest form, Creation usually refers to "God creating the universe and everything within it." But there are some distinctions:

- *Young earth creationism* (also known as creation science, scientific creationism): The Genesis account refers to six 24-hour days. Counting by the genealogies of the Bible, the Creation process commenced about 10,000 years ago.

- *Old earth creationism:* The "days" of Genesis are not six literal 24-hour days, but Creation did occur in the order specified in Genesis. The universe is billions of years old.

In chapter 4 we will talk more about the "old earth" versus "young earth" controversy.

Darwinism (also known as neo-Darwinism, evolutionism): The belief that undirected mechanistic processes (primarily random mutations and natural selection) can account for both microevolution and macroevolution, and thus for all the diverse and complex living organisms that exist. A key philosophical component of Darwinism is the assumption that "evolution works without either plan or purpose." The National Association of Biology Teachers Statement of 1996 referred to it as "an unsupervised, impersonal, unpredictable, and natural process."

Evolution: Evolution is an unplanned and undirected process; it combines elements of random genetic changes or mutations which are accumulated through natural selection. But it is important to distinguish between the two types of evolution. We've been through this several times before. You know it as well as we do by now, so say it with us...

- *Microevolution:* Evolution at and below the species level. It generally refers to relatively minor variations that occur in a group over time.

- *Macroevolution:* This is evolution above the species level. It generally refers to major innovations such as new organs, structures, or body plans.

Intelligent design: The earth, life, and humanity owe their existence to a purposeful, intelligent Creator. Darwinism is usually held to be incompatible with intelligent design.

Naturalism: The theory of naturalism denies that any event or object has supernatural significance; scientific laws are adequate to account for all phenomena.

What's That Again?

1. Until 150 years ago, the predominant view in Western culture was that God created the heavens and the earth.

2. In 1859 Charles Darwin wrote *On the Origin of Species*, which proposed that the universe came about through undirected natural causes. His theory of common descent taught that all life on Earth came from a common ancestor.

3. The lack of fossil evidence and the presence of irreducible complexity in life-forms weaken Darwinism.

4. The theory of intelligent design, which claims that an intelligent cause is necessary to explain the complex objects and structures in the universe,

has recently begun to challenge Darwinism in the scientific community.

5. Intelligent design doesn't stifle scientific investigation. On the contrary, it operates within the scope of science.

6. If we limit our scientific investigations to a framework of undirected natural causes, then science will be incapable of investigating God's interaction with the world. But if we permit science to investigate intelligent design, then God's interaction with the world becomes a legitimate domain for scientific investigation.

Dig Deeper

We've got four great books to recommend to you that deal with the debate between Darwinists and intelligent design:

The classic is *Darwin on Trial* by Phillip E. Johnson. This book gives an excellent presentation of the misleading claims of Darwinism and the tactics used by its supporters to conceal those weaknesses.

Phillip Johnson is a brilliant attorney. (Not all lawyers are. Bruce is proof of that.) But in his book *Defeating Darwinism by Opening Minds,* he explains in an easy-to-understand fashion the problems with Darwin's evolutionary theory. If you are looking for an introductory book, this would be a good choice.

Mere Creation is not a beginner's book. It contains the papers presented by scientists at a research conference for scientists and scholars who reject naturalism for the framework of science. This is one of the first texts that gave definition to the intelligent design movement. The editor is William A. Dembski. This book may be a bit too technical for you unless you are in the running for a Nobel prize for work in microbiology (or at least won "honorable mention" at the science fair).

Intelligent Design by William A. Dembski is the classic book for those interested in intelligent design theory. It explains that the fast-growing intelligent design movement is three things: a scientific research program for investigating intelligent causes, an intellectual program that challenges naturalistic evolutionary theories, and a way of understanding divine action.

◩ ◩ ◩

*Q*uestions for *R*eflection and *D*iscussion

1. In your own words, describe Darwin's theory of common descent.

2. What is the difference between *microevolution* and *macroevolution*? Give a real-life example of microevolution. That won't be so easy with macroevolution (because none have ever been proven), but cite some common illustrations that are often used to explain this theory.

3. What did Darwin expect would be found—eventually—in the fossil record (once paleontology techniques got sophisticated enough)? Nothing like Darwin was looking for has turned up in the last 150 years. How does that affect your response to the theory of macroevolution?

4. Explain how the *principle of irreducible complexity* is a threat to the theories of common descent and macroevolution.

5. Describe the *principle of intelligent design*.

6. The Intelligent Design movement is not just a bunch of scientists who are Christians. It includes scientists from many different religious faiths. And it also includes agnostic scientists who have no religious convictions. How can there be so much diversity on theological issues within this scientific perspective?

7. Give some examples of scientific occupations that recognize the possibility of an outside or third party cause. (We'll get you started: crime-scene investigators and coroners find a dead body and look at the evidence to determine if the death was caused naturally or by an outside influence.)

8. Do you agree with the Darwinists that its scientific inquiry should be limited to undirected, random processes of nature and that the possibilities of intelligent design should be disregarded because it is non-intellectual? Explain your answer.

□   □   □

Moving On...

Darwin gave us a Creation story, one in which God was absent and undirected natural processes did all the work. That Creation story has held sway for more than a hundred years. But it is now on the way out as proponents of intelligent design chip away at the foundations of Darwinism.

But the debate between Darwinists and proponents of intelligent design isn't the only debate going on. There is one that seems to be going on between people on the same side. Actually, it is a very heated debate which can distract you from the real issue of "God" or "no God." In chapter 4 we'll give you an insider's view of this ancillary debate—just enough so you'll know what it's about but not so much that you get bogged down on the wrong issues.

Chapter 4

To see a World in a Grain of Sand,
And a Heaven in a Wild Flower,
Hold Infinity in the palm of your hand,
And Eternity in an Hour.

—*William Blake*

Most fairy tales start with the opening words, "Once upon a time." When we hear that beginning to any story, we automatically assume we are about to hear a story someone made up.

A lot of people—including some who believe in God—believe that the beginning of the Bible starts with "Once upon a time" rather than "In the beginning." Even if you were to correct them, they would still think the story of Creation that follows is more fairy tale than truth.

We're here to say (along with some other highly credible people) that the beginning of the Bible is a story of fact, not fiction. And even though everyone doesn't agree on *when* the events of Creation took place, we can agree on *who* was responsible and *how* it happened. That's what this chapter is all about.

Once upon a Time

*T*ime can be very confusing. Depending on the context, the word *time* can mean a lot of different things:

- **Do you have the time?** This is a question people will ask you from time to time. Even though you don't actually have time like you might have a wristwatch or an apple, you gladly give the time to the person asking. Of course, you aren't really giving time away—it's not yours to give! All you can do is tell someone what time it is, and you can do this only if you have a wristwatch (an apple is completely useless). And think about this: Just when you think you have the exact time, that time is already in the past.

- *I ran out of time!* We all say this, but can you really run out of time? Time isn't like gasoline, where you really can run out and have to get more before your life can go on. To "run out of time" means that we didn't finish the project or the test in the time allotted. There's always more time because time doesn't stop. It keeps going and going and going...

- *Next time we'll stop for gas.* Now this is an interesting one. This has nothing to do with seconds and minutes and hours, the measurements of time. What you're saying here is that when this situation comes up again, you will respond in a different manner (unless you're a guy, in which case you will probably say something like, "Trust me, I know what I'm doing.")

See what we mean? The word *time* is relative. And so is time itself. Take time zones as an example. We live in the Pacific Time Zone. Let's say you live in the Eastern Time Zone. That means it's 9:00 A.M. where we are when it's noon your time. The farther two different time zones get from each other, the bigger the time difference. And when you cross the international date line, you go into an entirely different *day*.

Time can refer to a single moment ("The time is now 7:43"), a set period of time ("You will have plenty of time to finish the test"), or an indefinite event ("Tell me when it's time to go").

In the Beginning

Just like *time,* the words *begin* and *beginning* can have different meanings, depending on the way they are used:

- When will you *begin* your new job?

- It's *beginning* to rain.

- From small *beginnings* come great things.

The Theory of Relativity

We won't even begin to explain Einstein's theory of relativity, which revolutionized science in the twentieth century, but we will make this observation based on one thing we know about it. One of the things Einstein discovered is that the speed of light is constant, and that the speed is 186,000 miles per second. He theorized that time slows down relative to speed, and when speed equals the speed of light, time ceases altogether.

You can even use *time* and *begin* in combination. Try this on for size: There's always *time* to *begin* again.

We are perfectly content to give the concepts of "time" and "beginning" plenty of room when it comes to our everyday lives and experiences. We are flexible because we know it's next to impossible to sharply define when things begin and how long things take. "Hold on there," you might be saying. "I can tell you when I *began*. I was born on such-and-such a date at such-and-such a *time*."

Oh really? You mean to say your life began when you were born? Aren't you being a little presumptuous? What about all that time in your mother's womb? And just exactly when were you conceived anyway? You're too embarrassed to ask your parents, and even if you did, they probably wouldn't know.

So we're willing to be a little flexible with each other when it comes to time and beginnings, but when it comes to God and the Bible and how it all began, we can become very rigid. We want to know exactly when the world began. If we could, we would like to assign a date to the beginning of the world. (Believe it or not, someone already did. You'll read about that later in the chapter.)

Think about this for a minute (you don't have to time yourself—*minute* is a relative term): If our human perspective on time and beginnings is anything but exact, who are we to assign exact parameters for the eternal perspective on the beginning of time?

Yet that's exactly what we do. We may be ten minutes late for church and think nothing of it, but we want to know for sure that the beginning of the universe took place exactly _____ years ago (insert your own number). Furthermore, we want to be absolutely sure that God took exactly _____ days or _____ years to create everything in the universe.

The Slug and the Gardener

Use your imagination for a moment. We are the creation and God is the Creator. As C. S. Lewis once observed, we are like slugs in the garden, and God is the Master of the garden (only the difference between us and God is a lot bigger than that). So the slugs are telling the Master, "Excuse me, Master, we may be lowly slugs, but we know all about you. We know *when* you do stuff and we know *why* you do stuff. Just thought you would like to know that we know. It makes us feel so much better to know."

Okay, we think we've made our point (and we hope you get it). We really are the slugs of the universe, and God really is the Master of the universe. We can speculate about things that aren't clear (like dates and time), but it's ridiculous for us slugs to claim complete knowledge about them. God wants us to *know* Him, but He doesn't expect us to always *understand* Him. If God were talking to us right now, do you know what He would say?

> *"My thoughts are completely different from yours," says the* Lord. *"And my ways are far beyond anything you could imagine. For just as the heavens are higher than the earth, so are my ways higher than your ways and my thoughts higher than your thoughts"* (Isaiah 55:8-9).

And that's what He did say, right there in the Bible. Pretty convincing, isn't it? You see, God isn't being arrogant (although He would have every right to be). He's just being God. He's basically saying, "I'm God and you're not." That's the trouble with so many people today. They don't just want to know God. They want to figure God out. Even more, they want to be like God and know everything there is to know, both good and evil (now where have we heard that before?).

His Time Isn't Our Time

God's ways are not our ways, and His thoughts are not our thoughts. Is it too much of a stretch to believe that His time is not our time? God created time for our benefit, but He exists *outside* of the time dimension. Moses, who wrote the Book of Genesis, understood this concept very well. Here's what he wrote about God and His time:

For you, a thousand years are as yesterday! They are like a few hours! (Psalm 90:4).

So Why Are We Arguing?

Isn't it amazing? People who don't have a personal relationship with God are debating the big issues, such as the nature of God and the reality of God in our world. On the other hand, people who believe in God seem to be arguing about minor matters, such as the color of the carpet in the church or the date for the creation of the world.

Rather than talking with people who have real questions about who God is, we're arguing with each other about what God did and when He did it. Rather than studying the Bible as God's source for truth, we are forming opinions that are nowhere to be found in the Bible—and we're holding onto them as if our lives depended on it.

Do you see what is happening?

- Those who don't follow God and don't believe the Bible is the source of all truth are debating the *origins* of the universe. Many know there is a beginning (see chapter 1), they are even willing to admit there is a *beginner*. The issue they are dealing with is whether or not this beginner is an impersonal source or the personal God of the Bible. They want to know *who*.

- Those who follow God and believe the Bible are debating the *timing* of the universe. They know there is a Creator, but they aren't content to focus on the *who*. They want to know *when*.

We aren't suggesting that Christians shouldn't talk about when the universe began (we are devoting most of this chapter to the when). But we shouldn't let our debates over a secondary issue overshadow or interfere with the more important primary issue: who.

What Does the Bible Say?

The Bible is the world's most remarkable book for one simple reason: God wrote it. Well, to clarify, God didn't write the Bible the way we write books (that's a relief). As we explain in *Knowing the Bible 101*, God breathed into (Bible word: *inspired*) 40 different human authors to write down His message (2 Timothy 3:16). Because of this process, you can trust the Bible completely. God, who is perfect, used a foolproof means to get His message into print. He "breathed" into them and got what He wanted. Nothing more, nothing less.

This match between Bible and science would really be quite surprising if the Bible were merely ancient guesswork or made-up stories. But the fit between them is just the sort of thing we might expect if the God who created the universe was also behind the Bible.

—Robert C. Newman

So what does the Bible say about the *who*, the *when*, and the *how* of Creation, which includes the beginning of the universe and the "days" of Creation? First, there are three Creation accounts in the Bible: Genesis 1, Genesis 2, and Psalm 104.

Genesis 1:1–2:4	The original account of the events of Creation
Genesis 2:4-25	The Creation account from a different perspective

| *Psalm 104* | A poetic version of the Creation account told by King David |

Who

When you read these chapters carefully, you will notice that the greatest emphasis is on the *who* of Creation. In Genesis 1:1–2:4 the name *God* and the pronoun *He* are used 36 times in 35 verses. In Genesis 2:4-25, the name *Lord God* and the pronoun *He* are used 15 times. In Psalm 104, David used the names *God, Lord,* and *Spirit* 14 times. The personal pronouns *You* and *Your* are used 48 times. Clearly the *who* of Creation is the most important issue.

There's no question that God—speaking through Moses in Genesis and David in the Psalms—wants us to know that He is the one responsible for the universe, our world, and our lives. He is to be praised above all.

> *Praise the Lord, I tell myself; O Lord my God, how great you are! You are robed with honor and with majesty; you are dressed in a robe of light. You stretch out the starry curtain of the heavens; you lay out the rafters of your home in the rain clouds. You make the clouds your chariots; you ride upon the wings of the wind. The winds are your messengers; flames of fire are your servants. You placed the world on its foundation so it would never be moved. (Psalm 104:1-5).*

How

Next in importance is the *how* of Creation. The Bible is not a scientific book, and God didn't inspire the human authors to write in scientific terms. But as you have already seen in chapter 2 (and will see in greater detail in Part Two), the Bible is an accurate and trustworthy book 100 percent of the time and in every way, whether you are dealing with science, history, or your personal life. Nothing in the text of Genesis 1 and 2 contradicts the latest scientific discoveries. Remember our statement in chapter 1? Here it is again: *The more we learn about how the universe began and how it works, the more the universe points to God.*

So How Did God Make the Universe?

Remember our Latin lesson in chapter 1? *Ex nihilo nihil fit* means that you can't get something from nothing. When you refer to the act of God creating the universe, there is another Latin phrase: *creatio ex nihilo,* which means "created out of nothing." That's what God did. He created the universe out of nothing. As we explained in chapter 1, God is the only being capable and qualified to do this because He is the only being who is self-existent. God has always existed, which means He existed *before* the beginning.

As to how God accomplished this, here is another fancy foreign word: by *fiat.* No that doesn't mean he used a foreign sports car. It means that God created the universe by simply commanding it. Here's what the Bible says:

> *By faith we understand that the entire universe was formed at God's command, that what we now see did not come from anything that can be seen* (Hebrews 11:3).

When you go back to Genesis, you can clearly read that God said "Let there be light," and there was light (Genesis 1:3). God said, "'Let there be space between the waters, to separate water from water.' And so it was" (Genesis 1:6-7). In other words, all God had to do was say the word!

When

After the *who* and the *how,* the Bible talks about the *when,* but not in a way that makes it easy to determine. We've already given you examples in English of how the word *beginning* can mean different things. The same thing is true in Hebrew, the original language of Genesis (which means "beginning" by the way) and the entire Old Testament.

The root word of *beginning* is "first," but the meaning isn't restricted to the "first moment." It's much more indefinite. Old Testament scholar and Hebrew language expert John Sailhamer writes:

> Since the Hebrew word translated "beginning" refers to an indefinite period of time, we cannot say for certain when God created the world or how long He took to create it. This period could have spanned as much as several billion years, or it could have been much less; the text simply does not tell us how long. It tells us only that God did it during the "beginning" of our universe's history.

When you get to the word *day* in Genesis 1 and 2, the original Hebrew is even less definite. Just as the word *day* can have different meanings in English, so it has three different meanings in Hebrew which indicate three different periods of time:

- *Sunrise to sunset.* The Hebrew word for *day* in Genesis 1 and 2 can refer to a 12-hour period of time. The same meaning can be used in English, as in "I worked all *day*." You aren't saying that you worked for 24 hours. You just put in a full day's work.

- *Sunset to sunset.* The Hebrew word can also refer to a 24-hour period of time. This would be the same as if you said, "There are only three more days until my birthday."

- *A period of time not related to the sun.* Here the Hebrew word for *day* can refer to anything from a few weeks to a year to an age. Again, our English word *day* can have this same meaning. Have you ever heard an old person say, "In my day we didn't have fancy conveniences like running water"? You get the idea.

*G*od and the Theory of Relativity

A few pages back we talked about the theory of relativity and how time stands still at the speed of light. Okay, based on that, here's something to ponder. How fast is God? Pretty fast. More than pretty fast. God is infinitely fast. At least as fast as light and probably faster. (Isn't it interesting how many times the Bible refers to God and Jesus in terms of light?)

This means that for God, time stands still. Not only are a thousand years like a few hours (Psalm 90:4), but an infinite number of years are like a few hours.

Perhaps the best way to understand this is to see that God dwells outside the dimension of time. He created time for our benefit, not His. God exists in the eternal present. When Moses asked God to describe Himself, here is what God said: "I AM THE ONE WHO ALWAYS IS" (Exodus 3:14).

When Jesus told the people that He had seen Abraham, even though Abraham had been dead for thousands of years, Jesus explained: "I existed before Abraham was even born!" (John 8:58). On the surface, that statement doesn't make much sense. But when you realize that Jesus is God, and that God is eternally present, it makes complete sense. It also helps us understand God's infinite nature when it comes to time.

Does Anybody Really Know What Time It Is?

So what's the bottom line on this issue of time and Creation? Here it is. Are you ready? Drumroll, please.

- *We know the who.* There is no disputing the First Big Cause. There is only one Beginner, only one Originator, only one self-existent Creator. There is only one God; there is no other (Isaiah 45:5-6). When the Bible says that "God created the heavens and the earth" (Genesis 1:1), it is a completely true statement. There can be no doubt.

- *We know the how.* Only God could merely "say the word" and create the universe. Only God is that powerful, that infinite, and that loving to make something so perfect for us. "By faith we understand that the entire universe was formed at God's command, that what we now see did not come from anything that can be seen" (Hebrews 11:3).

- **We don't know the when.** We can debate and we can speculate, but the bottom line is this: We just don't know exactly *when* the *who* did the *how*. But we can take comfort in this. Not knowing exactly when the incredible beginning of the universe occurred takes nothing away from God and His plan for the universe (which includes you, by the way).

There are some essential things about God and the world and us that we must agree on if we are to call ourselves "believers" in the one true God of the Bible. We like to call these the "Five Essential Beliefs":

1. God created the universe and everything in it, including human beings, whom He created in His image (Genesis 1–2).

2. Sin and death (the consequence of sin) infected the entire human race when we disobeyed God and turned to our own ways, thereby separating us from God (Genesis 3; Isaiah 53:6; Romans 5:12).

3. God's eternal plan is to save us from the consequences of sin and to bring us back into relationship with Him through His only Son, Jesus Christ, who is fully God and fully man. The only way to God is through the life, death, and resurrection of Jesus Christ (John 3:16; 14:6; Romans 3:21-24; 1 Corinthians 15:3).

4. The Bible is the completely true and completely trustworthy word of God, inspired by God and useful to teach us everything we need to know about Him and how we should live (2 Timothy 3:16). That does not mean, however, that we know everything about God and His ways.

5. Jesus is at the right hand of God preparing a place for us in heaven. At some future time known only by God, Jesus Christ will return to Earth to gather all who believe

in Him, both the dead and the living, to join Him in heaven. Jesus will defeat all the enemies of God, and God will judge all who rejected His only plan to save humankind (John 14:1-4; 1 Corinthians 15:20-24; 1 Thessalonians 4:15-18; Revelation 20:11-15).

Once you get past these Five Essential Beliefs, you quickly get to some very important but nonessential beliefs.* Some of these nonessentials may be near and dear to your heart, but they're not worth dying for (we mean this in both a figurative and literal sense). And your point of view in a nonessential belief area should not come between you and a fellow believer to the point that you destroy a friendship.

We're not going to go through a list of these nonessential beliefs (trust us, there are more than five), but we are going to tell you that the *when* of Creation is among them. It's okay to have a viewpoint about the timing of Creation (in fact, we encourage it), but don't for a minute believe that your standing before God depends on your viewpoint, and don't ever let it come between you and your Christian friends (hey, we don't even want your viewpoint on when the world began to come between you and your non-Christian friends, but more about that at the end of the chapter).

Three Views of the When of Creation

Keeping that in mind, we want to give you the three major views of what the Bible means when it says, "In the beginning God created the heavens and the earth." Before we do, we want to make sure you understand that each of these three views includes the following "essential" beliefs:

- God created the universe.

- The Bible is the completely true Word of God.

- Our knowledge of God and His ways is incomplete.

---

* What we mean by "nonessential" is that these beliefs have nothing to do with God saving us through Jesus Christ. That is not to say that the other beliefs we have are not important for living as Christ-followers in a world that has rejected Him.

Young Earth Creationism

This is the view that God created the universe approximately 6000 to 10,000 years ago in a period of six literal 24-hour days. The reason the earth "looks" much older than it is can be explained primarily by Noah's global flood (Genesis 6–8), which dramatically changed the geology of the earth. For example, rather than being formed over millions of years through gradual erosion, the Grand Canyon was formed in a period of weeks or months by the rapid and powerful receding waters of Noah's flood.

As for the measurement of light that would seem to indicate an old universe, young earth creationists claim the speed of light was much faster just after Creation than it is now. This means that light from distant galaxies got here "right away" rather than over a period of billions of years.

Young earth creationists interpret the Creation account in Genesis 1 and 2 literally. They prefer a "probable" reading of the Bible—in other words, take it for what it says—even if it contradicts a more "plausible" scientific picture of an old earth. Furthermore, science is always changing. What we believe to be true today may not be true tomorrow (remember that scientists once suggested bleeding patients as a cure for disease).

Which View Is the Oldest?

You may be wondering which view of Creation has been around the longest. According to both Dr. Hugh Ross and Fred Heeren, the early church fathers believed the Creation days were not necessarily "solar days." In the second century, Clement of Alexandria taught that the Genesis creation days were not literal 24-hour days. He believed that the order of the Creation days was more important than the time frame. In the fourth century, Augustine believed that the "evenings and mornings" of Genesis were figurative, not literal. They weren't considered literally until the seventeenth century, when John Lightfoot of Cambridge and James Ussher of Ireland competed to come up with an exact date for the beginning of Creation.

Basing their calculations on the genealogies of the King James Version of the Bible (published in 1611), Lightfoot and Ussher counted the generations backwards from Jesus to Adam. Ussher arrived at October 4, 4004 B.C. as the date of Creation, which Lightfoot later corrected to

October 18, 4004 B.C. One of the problems with the work of these two men was in the genealogies themselves. Bible scholars have demonstrated that the Bible doesn't include *every* generation in the genealogies, which means that basing dates on the number of generations in the Bible isn't a reliable method.

Old Earth Creationism

Also known as "progressive" creationism, this view teaches that God created the universe 10 to 15 billion years ago. Some old earth creationists believe the "days" of Creation in Genesis 1 and 2 are long periods of time (day-age view), while others believe that each "day" of Creation was a literal 24-hour day separated by long periods of time (gap or intermittent-day view).

While the Bible doesn't give us the age of the earth or the universe, it does tell us that time is different for God than for man (Psalm 90:4; 1 John 2:18). Furthermore, the scientific evidence seems to point more and more to an old universe. Old earth creationists cite light as an example. Because the light we see from stars has traveled across space at a rate of 186,000 miles per second, astronomers measure the distance light travels in light-years. The most distant galaxies are ten billion light-years away, which means that the universe is at least ten billion years old.

Creation of Humans in God's Image

There is another very essential thing that both young earth and old earth creationists agree on, and that's the fact that humans are created in the image of God (Genesis 1:26-27). This separates us from all other living creatures and means we have a unique relationship with our Creator and very special responsibilities for the creation. Young and old creationists also agree that God created Adam and Eve, the first humans made in God's image, several thousand years ago. (There will be more about the creation of humans in God's image in chapter 8.)

Theistic Evolution

Also known as "the fully gifted creation" by the movement's chief proponent, Howard Van Till, this view attempts to bring together the concepts of "divine creation" (theism) and "biotic evolution" (naturalism) in a way that glorifies God and preserves the integrity of science. In a nutshell, theistic evolutionists believe that God created human beings by means of evolution and natural selection. Although they believe the Bible is true, they interpret the Creation account in the Bible in a figurative sense.

What About Our View?

Well, for one thing, we believe we were created in God's image and for His glory. We also believe that you are free to have any view of Creation you choose, as long as you think it through and stay consistent with the essential beliefs we talked about earlier. Here are some other things we believe about Creation. (We are giving you these not to sway you to our viewpoint, but to provide a framework for the rest of this book.)

1. The universe definitely had a beginning, as the Bible has always said and as science has now confirmed (see chapter 1).

2. Science has also confirmed that we live in a universe that has been "finely tuned" to an incredibly precise extent. There is no explanation for this fine-tuning except to say an intelligent designer created the universe (see chapter 3).

3. It is becoming more and more evident that our earth is just as finely tuned as the universe, to the extent that even nontheists are having to admit that the earth and its inhabitants are unique in the universe (see chapter 6).

4. The "witness" of the earth—whether you are studying geology, biology, physics, or astronomy—seems to point more and more to an old earth. Robert C. Newman writes, "Here we have the convergent testimony of several diverse witnesses agreeing on an old earth."

5. The idea of an old earth does not contradict Scripture or compromise the truth about God in any way.

6. The old earth creationist view, especially when it is coupled with the idea of intelligent design, is fully compatible with scientific truth.

The Real Issue

We think you know the real issue of how it all began. The real issue is not the age of the universe or the length of Creation days. The real issue is much bigger and much more important. *The real issue is God.* Either He created the heavens and the earth or He didn't.

In the public school system, on the university campus, in the office, or on the playing field, people want to know this more than any other issue, because it leads them to a very personal question: **Is God Real?**

You need to be about the business of telling people that God is real—both in your life and in the world. And it all starts with being certain in your own mind about why God is real.

- God is real in the world because He made the world (Romans 1:20).

- God is real in your life because He made you in His image (Genesis 1:26-27).

- God has given you a real life and real hope because He made you into a new person through Jesus Christ (2 Corinthians 5:17).

You may not be certain about all of these things right now. That's okay! There's nothing wrong with doubt, as long as you are truthfully seeking God for who He is, not for who you want Him to be. Be patient. God has promised to reward "those who sincerely seek him" (Hebrews 11:6).

If you're certain about God, but you have some doubts about some "nonessential" issues, that's okay, too! You're never going to figure God out completely, which is part of the joy and excitement of the Christian life. As you seek God, He will reward you by giving you insights into His truth. The Bible says:

> *If you need wisdom—if you want to know what God wants you to do—ask him, and he will gladly tell you. He will not resent your asking* (James 1:5).

Don't let side issues get in the way of the real issue. Don't give anyone seeking the real God a reason to wonder if God is real. Instead, "if you are asked about your Christian hope, always be ready to explain it" (1 Peter 3:15).

"What's That Again?"

1. The words *time* and *beginning* can have different meanings, both in our language and in Hebrew, the original language of the Old Testament.

2. We must be careful about wanting to know everything there is to know about God and His ways. Many things about God are simply beyond our ability to understand.

3. While those who don't follow God are debating whether or not God created the universe, those who know God are debating when the universe was created.

4. The Bible is very clear about *who* created the universe and *how* it happened. The Bible is not clear about *when* it happened and how long it took.

5. As long as we agree on the essential things about God and the world and us, we can respectfully disagree on the nonessential issues.

6. There are basically three views of Creation: young earth creationism, old earth creationism, and theistic evolution. We favor the old earth Creation view.

7. The real issue is Creator versus no Creator. This leads to the real question: Is God real?

Dig Deeper

The best book we found on the issue of creation and time is *Creation and Time* by Dr. Hugh Ross. Even though Dr. Ross is a Mensa member (that means he's very, very smart), he has a clear and compassionate style that doesn't ridicule those who would disagree with him.

Dr. John Sailhamer's book *Genesis Unbound* looks at the Creation account from the perspective of language and Old Testament history. Unfortunately, this book is out of print.

Three Views on Creation and Evolution is an excellent (if a bit difficult) book on the three viewpoints we presented in this chapter. The reason it's difficult is that the writers are true scholars (unlike us). In true debate style, each view is presented and then rebutted.

◻ ◻ ◻

*Q*uestions for *R*eflection and *D*iscussion

1. Describe in as much detail as you can the time when you were born. Where were you born? What was the name of the hospital? What time of day were you born? What was the weather like? Did anything unusual happen on the day you were born? (If you have trouble remembering, call the person who would know best.)

2. Why do you think people want so badly to define God, quantify God, and explain how, why, and when God does things?

Why hasn't God been more self-revealing about His thoughts and His ways?

3. What would happen if people who have a personal relationship with God were to stop arguing about *when* God created the universe and started debating the big issues—such as the reality of God and His nature—with people who don't know God personally?

4. Read the three creation accounts in the Bible: Genesis 1:1–2:4; Genesis 2:4-25; Psalm 104. How are these the same? How are they different?

5. Explain this statement: "For God, time stands still." Can you show this to be true from Scripture? How about science?

6. Review the Five Essential Beliefs. What beliefs, if any, would you add to this list?

7. Which of the three views of the *when* of creation comes closest to what you believe? How did you arrive at your belief? Do you respect the other viewpoints?

Moving On...

Congratulations! You've made it through the all-important "setup" for this book on how it all began. If you're reading this for the science, you're probably glad we finally got past some of the history and philosophy and theology and are ready to move on to the real meat of Creation.

If science isn't your strong suit, don't worry. We're not going to get so technical (we couldn't even if we tried) that you get lost in the process. As we say in every one of our books: If two guys like us can understand this stuff, then so can you.

The great thing about Part Two is that it's going to energize your faith. We really believe that. In Part One we talked about some of the recent scientific discoveries that point to the beginning and incredible fine-tuning of our universe. Now we're going to get more specific. We think you're going to find that the universe points to God in specific ways that will make you appreciate and love Him more specifically than you thought possible.

$\mathcal{P}$art II
God Created the Heavens and the Earth

Chapter 5

The Christian doctrine of creation is consonant with the Big Bang and can justifiably be regarded as a better explanation of the Big Bang than its naturalistic competitors. In the competition with naturalism, divine creation comes out the champion.

—*William Dembski*

Some of the most remarkable scientific discoveries of the last century have been made by astronomers looking at the heavens through high-powered telescopes and sophisticated cameras mounted on satellites designed to probe the depths of space. When the psalmist wrote, "The heavens tell of the glory of God" (Psalm 19:1), could he have imagined how far into the heavens we could actually see? Could he have known then what scientists know now—that the evidence from space points in great detail to a personal, intelligent designer rather than an impersonal, undirected process?

The recent discoveries in space—especially those made in big-bang science—are convincing many former skeptics to at least consider the role of a supernatural Creator in the beginning and development of the universe. Writing in *U.S. News & World Report*, Gregg Easterbrook reported that Allan Sandage, one of the world's top astronomers, recently told fellow cosmologists that "contemplating the majesty of the big bang helped make him a believer in God, willing to accept that creation could only be explained as a 'miracle.'"

You may not be an astronomer—hey, you may never have even looked through a telescope—but you cannot help wondering about stuff that no other generation in the history of the world has seen. It's enough to make you see stars!

God's Big Bang

*W*hat do you think of when you hear the words "big bang?" Does it bring to mind—

- a false, almost sacrilegious explanation of how the world began;

- a simple but basically accurate picture of the first split second of the beginning of the universe; or

- that annoying noise your car makes when it backfires?

If the very idea of a big bang makes you cringe, don't worry. You've got plenty of company. The concept of the big bang makes a lot of people uncomfortable. But you might be surprised at who finds the big bang theory threatening.

- On the one hand you have some creationists who put the big bang on the same shelf as Darwinism, because they believe the big bang automatically rules out the purposeful action of a Creator.

- On the other hand you have some Darwinists who reject the idea of a big bang because it implies a beginning, which inevitably leads to a Creator, and that's something they cannot and will not admit.

Do you see the big bang picture here? You have some creationists and some Darwinists who reject the big bang, but for exactly the opposite reasons. So who's right? Well, this may be the only time in this book that you'll hear us say this, but here it goes: The Darwinists are right. Not in their conclusions, but in their understanding of where the big bang leads! As you're going to see in this chapter, the big bang leads you to—and not away from—the necessity of a Creator.

What Is the Big Bang?

To show you what we mean, here are two definitions of the big bang. The first is from Professor John Wiester, a physical scientist, a proponent of intelligent design, and the science adviser for this book:

> Most scientists now believe that our universe was created quite suddenly and abruptly more than 15 billion years ago in a cataclysmic explosion termed the Big Bang. In the initial cosmic fireball, energy was converted into matter and the results flung far out into the void to construct, in effect, atoms, molecules, bases, stars, planets, and space itself. All the matter and energy in the universe, including the physical elements of which you and I are composed, had their beginnings in the cosmic fireball of creation.

And here is a definition from astronomer Robert Jastrow, who describes himself as "an agnostic in religious matters":

> The astronomical evidence proves that the Universe was created 15 billion years ago in a fiery explosion.... The seeds of everything that has happened in the Universe since were planted in that first instant; every star, every planet and every living creature in the Universe owes its physical origins to events that were set in motion in the moment of the cosmic explosion. In a purely physical sense, it was the moment of creation.

Note how both definitions use the words *created* and *creation*. This is ironic, because unlike those who embrace intelligent design, Darwinists are reluctant to admit there was a personal, purposeful "Creator" involved. But they can't deny the fact that there was a First Big Cause that started it all. They just don't know what that Cause was.

You Can't See God Through a Telescope

Both Wiester and Jastrow admit that science cannot "prove" that God created the heavens and the earth, because as Jastrow puts it, "In the searing heat of that first moment, all the evidence needed for a scientific study of the cause of the great explosion was melted down and destroyed."

But just because science can't see God through a telescope doesn't mean that there isn't any evidence for His work. The whole idea of intelligent design is that the scientific evidence points to a purposeful, personal Creator, and not to an undirected, mechanical process. Even astronomer Fred Hoyle, one of the harshest critics of the big bang, had to admit, "A common-sense interpretation of the facts suggests that a superintellect has monkeyed with the physics."

So why are we spending all this time (and a whole chapter) talking about the big bang? What good does it do us if the big bang simply leads us to a First Big Cause, but doesn't tell us what or who the First Big Cause was?

Great question! And here's the answer. It's important to believe that "in the beginning God created the heavens and the earth." But it's also important for us to know *why* we believe. Let's say that someone asked you, "Why do you believe that God created the universe?" Here's one way you could respond: "I don't know the details, but I can tell you that the Bible says how it all began, so I believe it, and I don't need to know any more."

There's nothing wrong with that statement. On one level, your faith in God is simple enough for a child to understand. In fact, there is a point at which all of us—no matter how old or how smart—need to come to God "as little children." All we need to do is *believe* that what God said in His Word is true, and that's all there is to it. But there also comes a point in your Christian life when you need to grow and mature beyond a *simple* faith to a *reasonable* faith. When someone asks you about your Christian faith and the hope that it gives you, "always be ready to explain it" (1 Peter 3:15). That begins with explaining the Bible.

The apostle Paul, who was more knowledgeable about the Bible than anyone else in his time, wrote this to Timothy, who was a "child" in the faith:

> *Work hard so God can approve you. Be a good worker, one who does not need to be ashamed and who correctly explains the word of truth* (2 Timothy 2:15).

In our view, there's no better place to start explaining the word of truth than Genesis. Start with "in the beginning" and learn all you can about what that means. You're reading this book, which is terrific. This is going to be a great springboard for your study of how it all began. But we encourage you to keep studying about the Bible and science. The more you discover about Creation, the more you learn to appreciate the Creator. As David wrote more than 3000 years ago:

> *The heavens tell of the glory of God. The skies display his marvelous craftsmanship. Day after day they continue to*

speak; night after night they make him known (Psalm 19:1-2).

A Unique Place in History

From the time of David, who peered into the heavens with his naked eye, to the dawning of the twentieth century, science wasn't much help when it came to explaining how it all began. Astrophysicist George Smoot recently wrote, "Until the late 1910s, humans were as ignorant of cosmic origins as they had ever been. Those who didn't take Genesis literally had no reason to believe there had been a beginning."

Do you see what Dr. Smoot is saying? Until a hundred years ago, you had no reason to believe that God created the heavens and the earth except by faith. There was no way to explain it, scientifically or otherwise.

Then some very remarkable things began to happen in the world of science, especially in astronomy and physics. As we're going to show you in the next few pages, we now know things that help us explain what the Bible has said all along. As we said earlier, the scientific evidence doesn't tell us what or who caused the beginning, but it can tell us how.

Because of the work of some very smart people and the development of some timely technological advances, science has been able to construct a credible model for the beginning of the universe. It's taken nearly a hundred years, but here's the exciting part: *The most significant discoveries about how the universe began have occurred in your lifetime!*

No one before our time had the awesome privilege of seeing this stuff. King David, the apostle Paul, Saint Augustine, Martin Luther, Galileo, Newton, Einstein—all they could do was speculate about how the world began. But now we can actually know what happened because of what God has allowed us to see.

This is big—really big. This isn't, "Gee, now we can buy airline tickets over the Internet" big, or "Hey, look, they opened a new Starbucks in my neighborhood" big. This is cosmic origins big. This is *huge!*

ℒet's Review

In Part One of this book, we kicked off this whole thing by leading you down a very logical path to some very clear conclusions. Just in case you've forgotten, here's what we concluded:

1. The scientific evidence clearly demonstrates that the universe had a beginning.

2. If the universe had a beginning, there had to be a Beginner or First Big Cause which existed before the beginning.

3. Scientific naturalism and Darwinism assert that undirected mechanical processes can account for the universe and everything in it.

4. Creationism and the intelligent design theory assert that the universe and everything in it owes its existence to a purposeful, intelligent Creator.

5. The real issue is Creator or no Creator. "Is God real?" is the real question.

Amazing Discoveries of the Twentieth Century

Now let's take a little tour of the twentieth century (you remember the twentieth century, don't you?) from the standpoint of astronomy, physics, and ultimately, the big bang and the origins of the universe. As you read about these amazing discoveries, ask yourself a simple question: As these scientists peered into the heavens, did their discoveries and conclusions point toward a universe that was random and undirected, or was there a bigger plan and purpose at work? You make the call.

- **1914**—American astronomer Vesto Sipher (you just don't hear names like that these days) studied the speeds of the "nebulae" (that's what they called "galaxies" back then) as they moved through space. He found that most of the galaxies were moving away from the earth at high speeds.

- **1922**—Alexander Friedmann, a Russian mathematician, used Albert Einstein's equations of general relativity to speculate that the entire universe was expanding as galaxies moved away from each other.

What About Einstein?

The most famous and most influential scientific theory of the twentieth century was Albert Einstein's general theory of relativity, first published in 1915. We're not even going to begin to tell you what it's all about, because we don't know! However, we can tell you what it meant to other scientists trying to figure out how the universe began. Fred Heeren writes that "the equations of general relativity imply that the universe cannot be static, but must be expanding or contracting."

Ironically, at first Einstein didn't see the profound implication of his own theory. He thought the universe was static, and he incorrectly adjusted his equations accordingly. Alexander Friedmann found Einstein's error (which Einstein later called the biggest blunder of his career), proving that Einstein's "static" universe was "virtually impossible." Don't be too hard on Albert. Even with his "blunder," his theories paved the way for scientists throughout the twentieth century.

- **1927**—Georges Lemaitre, a Belgian astronomer, blended Einstein's equations and Friedmann's ideas. He concluded that if the universe was expanding, then it was once much smaller. In fact, Lemaitre believed that all the material in the universe had once been in a single place, "locked in a primordial atom of unthinkable mass."

- **1929**—Using the 100-inch Hooker telescope on top of Mount Wilson in California, American astronomer Edwin Hubble found what scientists believed but could not prove: Galaxies are rushing away from each other at high rates of speed. Not only that, but the farther away a galaxy is, the faster it moves. Here's what his findings meant. First, the universe is expanding. Second, everything in the universe came from a single, unbelievably

One Shift, Two Shift, Red Shift, Blue Shift

With apologies to Dr. Seuss (who never discovered anything astronomical), we need to explain a concept called "red shift," because it helped astronomers at the beginning of the twentieth century prove that the universe was expanding and finite rather than static and eternal.

You know what happens when light shines through a prism, right? The prism separates light into a spectrum of colors. Well, that's what Vesto Sipher did with the light from stars (the technique is called spectroscopy). Sipher understood that when light moves *away from* an observer, the light waves are *stretched* into longer wavelengths, making the light appear more red. In other words, the light shifts to the red side of the spectrum. By contrast, when light moves toward an observer from a source, the waves get shorter, making the light appear more blue. Sipher was surprised at how much "redshifting" he found in the nebulae he was observing, because it meant they were moving away from the observer and from each other.

Hubble used Sipher's work in redshifting to determine the distances of 24 nebulae (or galaxies) outside our own Milky Way galaxy.

powerful explosion. Astronomer Robert Jastrow calls this discovery, known as Hubble's law, one of the great discoveries of science and "one of the main supports of the scientific story of Genesis."

- **1946**—George Gamow, a Russian-born scientist, speculated that there was only one way for protons and neutrons to fuse together and form a perfectly balanced universe (one that is about three-fourths hydrogen and one-fourth helium). There had to be a rapid cooling from near infinitely high temperatures. In 1948, Gamow concluded that there had to have been an initial explosion of pure energy in order for matter to exist in the universe. Furthermore, Gamow proposed that this initial explosion was so strong that a "faint glow" of heat measuring 5 degrees Centigrade above absolute zero (that's –460 degrees Fahrenheit, which is even colder than Buffalo, New York, in the winter) should be found everywhere in the universe. Unfortunately, he didn't have the instruments to measure what he knew was there.

𝒯he Steady State Holds Steady

Not every scientist agreed with the idea that an expanding universe meant there was a beginning—and a rather explosive beginning at that (mainly because having a beginning implied a Beginner). British astronomer Fred Hoyle did his best to "prove" that the universe could expand and still have no beginning. His theory, which has never gained wide acceptance in the scientific community, was known as "steady state" cosmology. Nonetheless, as Robert Jastrow points out, "It is an appealing theory to the scientist, since it permits the contemplation of a universe without beginning and without end." Ironically, Hoyle was the one who gave the concept of the universe beginning with an incredible explosion a name: the big bang.

- **1965**—Two radio astronomers, Arno Penzias and Robert Wilson, proved what Gamow and others before him believed. Using equipment built in connection with a communications satellite project by AT&T Bell Laboratories, Penzias and Wilson measured the "faint glow" (known as "background radiation") Gamow had predicted. The "heat" they measured was so uniform that it could not have come from any single object in the sky, such as planets or stars. The entire universe seemed to be the source. The only explanation was that the universe was once superheated, and the only explanation for this was the "detonation" of a "primordial bang."

𝒯he Cosmic Oven

If all this business about background radiation and protons and neutrons fusing together is starting to fog your brain, join the club! This stuff can get a little complicated. Here's an illustration to help you understand the physics involved (it helped us a bunch). Astrophysicist Hugh Ross explains that the universe's beginning and development resembled a hot kitchen oven. When you open the door to a hot oven, the heat (or energy) trapped inside "radiates" into the kitchen and eventually the whole house. After a period of time, the oven itself cools down to the temperature of the house, which is now a few degrees warmer than it was before.

The universe is like the house, only a lot more finely tuned. In order for the proton and neutron elements in the universe to fuse together in exactly the right way, the expansion and the heat of the universe had to be just right, and that's exactly what happened. Everywhere scientists train their instruments, the universe contains similar heat and similar structures.

- **1992**—For scientists, the conclusive proof that we live in a uniform universe (astronomers call it a "homogeneous" universe) was evidence for a big bang beginning, but it wasn't enough. There was still one piece of the puzzle missing. If there was an explosion of unimaginable proportions that started it all, scientists believed that we should be able to measure the "ripples" that came from an explosive beginning (kind of like when you first open the door to a very hot oven). Until just a few years ago, there was no proof that those ripples existed because no one had the instruments to measure them. Then came the COBE satellite.

On April 24, 1992, a team of astrophysicists led by George Smoot at the University of California at Berkeley announced that the Cosmic Background Explorer (COBE) satellite had measured the ripples scientists had been looking for. Stephen Hawking, the world's most celebrated scientist, called it "the discovery of the century, if not of all time." Hugh Ross wrote that the COBE findings were a "stunning confirmation of the hot big bang creation event."

George Smoot declared, "What we have found is evidence for the birth of the universe. If you're religious, it's like looking at God."

It's like Looking at God

Very often, when scientists say things like George Smoot said (that looking at the origins of the universe is like "looking at God"), they aren't necessarily embracing a belief in the personal

The First Church of Christ of the Big Bang

In the wake of the COBE discovery, some scientists (and their numbers are dwindling) stubbornly refuse to accept the big bang model. Jeffrey Burbidge, a distinguished astrophysicist at the University of California at San Diego, complains that the COBE experiments come from "the first church of Christ of the big bang." Burbidge is essentially saying that if you buy into the big bang model, you must also buy into the story of Creation as found in the Bible (which is why Burbidge continues to support the "steady state" model, which is closer to Hinduism than theism). George Smoot, who is not a Christian, insists that his observations "were in no way colored by any religious presuppositions."

Creator of the universe, the God of the Bible. What they are saying is that the evidence for the birth of the universe points to a purposeful beginning rather than an "undirected, mechanical process." If you are "religious"—in other words, if you believe in God in one way or another—then for you it's like "looking at God." But if God is not a part of your belief system, then you aren't going to be too quick to give God the credit, even if you admit that something or someone caused the beginning.

Frederick Burnham, a science-historian, had this to say about the amazing discoveries of the twentieth century: "These findings, now available, make the idea that God created the universe a more respectable hypothesis today than at any time in the last 100 years." That's a nice statement, but saying that God is a "respectable hypothesis" isn't exactly saying that God created the universe.

---

*I*n 1962, astronaut John Glenn became the first American to orbit the earth. In 1998, at the age of 77, Senator John Glenn orbited the earth again on the space shuttle Discovery. When asked whether he prayed in space, here is how Glenn responded: "I pray every day in space, and I think everybody should. I don't think we can look at Earth every day, look down upon this kind of creation.... Not to believe in God is impossible."

British physicist Edmund Whittaker concluded, "There is no ground for supposing that matter and energy existed before and was suddenly galvanized into action. For what could distinguish that moment from all other moments in eternity? It is simpler to postulate creation *ex nihilo*—Divine will constituting Nature from nothingness." Here again, this scientist stops short of saying, "In the beginning God created the heavens and the earth." He's more comfortable referring to God as "Divine will."

Jeffrey Burbidge is right. We don't want to worship at the First Church of Christ of the Big Bang. Science and scientific discoveries are not the *end* of our search for God; they are simply part of the *means* to the end of truly knowing about God. The big bang is not God, and God is not the big bang. As we said in Part One, God is the self-existent, independent, supernatural, infinite, all-powerful God described in His own words in His own book, the Bible.

It's important that we go to the Bible to discover what God has said about the universe and how it all began. This is the only way to verify if this "respectable hypothesis" or "Divine will" or "intelligent designer" is the God of the Bible, and not just some being we have made up in order to satisfy our own inner cravings.

The Real World Series

Let's have some fun with this particular section. Rather than having a detailed discussion in a stuffy setting with Darwinists on one side and intelligent designers on the other, let's go outside and enjoy one of the greatest games ever invented. Let's play some baseball!

But this isn't just any baseball game. This is the Real World Series, because we've got two teams—the Darwinists and the Intelligent Designers—who will answer questions about the world and how it began. The winner will be the team who can best explain how the universe got here and what it means for the rest of us. Are you ready? Can you feel the excitement? Can you smell the popcorn? Can you picture the scene? Play ball!

First Up—the Darwinists

First up in the big inning (get it?—the *big inning*) are the Darwinists, an impressive team with a strong lineup of seasoned veterans. Until recently, the Darwinists have seemed unbeatable, but lately their confidence has been shaken. After a winning streak that stretched over many years, they have recently lost more games than they have won.

First up for the Darwinists is Alan Guth, who played college ball for MIT. Here's the first pitch: *We know that science has embraced the big bang model of the origin of the universe, but do you know who or what caused the big bang?*

Guth: "The big bang theory proposes no answer at all to the question of what banged, how it banged, or what caused it to bang."

And Guth grounds out with a dribbler down the first-base line. So you're saying, Dr. Guth, that there's no scientific evidence or explanation for what caused the big bang. Not very satisfying, is it?

Okay, who's your next batter? It looks like Andrei Linde from Stanford University. And here's the pitch: *Do you know where all the matter and energy in the universe came from? In other words, what really put the bang in the big bang?*

Linde: "You know, it is such an esoteric science, creation from nothing. You can come away with your interpretations and there is no way to check them. It is like a religion."

And it's a second out with an infield pop fly. Another Darwinist strikes out. If we understand this correctly, Dr. Linde, the big bang does not completely explain the origin of the universe. According to an article in *Astronomy* magazine, "Something had to happen *before* the big bang to get it going." That would seem like an impossible question for science to answer.

You have one more out. Do you have another batter? Oh, it looks like *two* batters: Neil Turok and Stephen Hawking, both mathematical physicists at Cambridge University. Fair enough. Here's the pitch: *Since you can't explain how the big bang happened, do you have any other theories, and is anybody buying them?*

Turok and Hawking: "We have this 'multiverse' theory, which basically says that multiple universes have been growing through a series of big bangs and will continue to grow eternally."

That's a big whiff as Turok and Hawking go down swinging! That's a big whiff! Sounds like a variation of the old oscillating theory of the universe, which the Hindu religion proposed centuries ago. Sorry, we can't accept that, and neither can your colleagues. There is no evidence to support your theory. They know that your theory suggests that the universe came from no tangible source. Even Dr. Turok admits his "preference" for what he calls a "one-shot" universe with "one beginning and one big bang."

There you have it. Three up and three down for the Darwinists. No runs, no hits, and no explanations.

Now Batting—the Intelligent Designers

Well, the top half of the big inning went quickly. Now it's the Intelligent Designers' turn to swing the lumber. This is a team that has been surprising everyone. They used to be cellar dwellers, but lately all the evidence has been going their way. The Intelligent Designers have some pretty impressive players. Let's see who's up first. It looks like William Dembski, a mathematician from the University of Chicago. Here's the pitch: *Why does intelligent design offer a better explanation for the beginning of the world than Darwinism (also known as naturalism)?*

Dembski: "Why should anyone want to understand the act of creation naturalistically? Naturalism, after all, offers fewer resources than theism. Naturalism simply gives you nature. Theism gives you not only nature but also God and anything outside of nature that God might have created. The ontology of theism is far richer than that of naturalism. Why then settle for less?"

Base hit. And Dembski's on base with a single up the middle. The Darwinists have admitted they cannot explain the cause of the big bang, because there's no evidence for what happened before the big bang. Furthermore, Darwinism can't explain God because God exists outside of nature.

The Intelligent Designers can explain the big bang, because God exists outside of nature and the universe. He is the only possible First Big Cause for the big bang and the universe that followed because only God exists outside of the four dimensions of the universe.

Now batting for the Intelligent Designers is Hugh Ross, who played for the University of Toronto and Cal Tech. And here's the pitch: *Intelligent design is a way of understanding divine action. What does intelligent design tell us about the designer?*

Ross: "Words such as *superintellect, monkeyed, overwhelming design, miraculous, ultimate purpose, supernatural Agency, supernatural plan, tailor-made, Supreme Being,* and *providentially crafted* obviously apply to a Person. Beyond just establishing that the Creator is a Person, the findings about design provide some evidence of what that Person is like."

Two-base hit. It's a double into left field for the wiry Ross. As you're going to see in chapter 6, the universe is so finely tuned that no naturalistic explanation seems adequate. MIT physicist Vera Kistiakowsky said, "The exquisite order displayed by our scientific understanding of the physical world calls for the divine." Dr. Ross points out that the Creator is a Person who cares for living things, particularly the human race: "We see this care in the vastness and quality of the resources devoted to life support."

All right, there are two men on, and coming to the plate is—wait a minute, we can't really see Him, but He's carrying an awfully big stick. Could it be? Yes, it appears that the next batter is the Designated Hitter, the Creator of the universe, the First Big Cause. It's God!

Uh, hello, God. We really only have one question. We know that all You had to do was speak and the heavens were created (Psalm 33:6). Did You stay involved with the whole process, or did You just let things take their natural course?

God: *Who is this that questions my wisdom with such ignorant words? Brace yourself, because I have some questions for you, and you must answer them. Where were you when I laid the foundations of the earth? Tell me, if you know so much. Do you know how its dimensions were determined and who did the surveying? What supports its foundations, and who laid its cornerstone as the morning stars sang together and all the angels shouted for joy? Who defined the boundaries of the sea as it burst from the womb, and as I clothed it with clouds and thick darkness? For I locked it behind barred gates, limiting its shores. I said, "Thus far and no farther will you come. Here your proud waves must stop!"* (Job 38:2-11).

Home run. Well, that pretty much clears the bases! And honestly, we don't have any more questions for God, at least not at this point.

God's Big Bang

Even though the big bang event didn't leave any direct evidence that it was God who caused it, we can draw two reasonable conclusions based on the evidence we do have:

1. The big bang event was not a random, undirected process. It was the purposeful act of an intelligent designer.

2. The only explanation for the identity of that intelligent designer is offered by the theistic worldview, which is based on the reality of a supernatural, transcendent God who exists outside the time and space dimensions of the universe.

The only other option is the naturalistic worldview (or Darwinism), which believes that the universe caused and created itself in perfect balance.

You see, with intelligent design and theism you get God as the ultimate reality. With Darwinism and naturalism all you get is nature. There's nothing outside our universe to account for its creation. Science and nature can tell us *what* happened at the instant of Creation, but they can't tell us *how.* Only the Bible offers an explanation, because only the Bible contains the words of God, who told us how He did it:

> *The LORD, your Redeemer and Creator, says: "I am the LORD, who made all things. I alone stretched out the*

heavens. By myself I made the earth and everything in it"
(Isaiah 44:24).

God "said the word" and the universe was born. But He did much more than that. He planned out every detail and carried it out in perfect order and balance. Go back and read the elegant, accurate explanation for the creation process in Genesis. When God said, "Let there be light," it wasn't like someone turned on a light switch in your house. Wiester writes, "The universe began at a sharply defined instant in time in a fiery explosion of intense brilliance. In the beginning, pure energy was transforming itself into matter."

This wasn't just any big bang. This was God's big bang which created God's universe. It was just the beginning of a process that got even more remarkable as the "days" of Creation unfolded.

"What's That Again?"

1. The universe was created at a single point in time around 15 billion years ago in a cataclysmic explosion of unimaginable proportions called the big bang.

2. Even though the big bang leads us to the First Big Cause, it doesn't tell us who the First Big Cause was. Yet a study of the big bang is useful because it helps us to understand why we believe that God created the heavens and the earth.

3. Until the 1920s, humans were as ignorant of cosmic origins as they ever had been. In the last century, scientists have discovered things about the universe that confirm what the Bible has said all along about how the universe began.

4. In 1992, scientists were able to measure the "ripples" that came from the explosive beginning of the universe, which Hugh Ross called a "stunning confirmation of the hot big bang event."

5. In light of the evidence, it is clear that the Bible and the concept of intelligent design offer a better explanation for cosmic origins than Darwinism.

Dig Deeper

William Dembski is one of the leading proponents of intelligent design. His book *Intelligent Design* offers a clear and reasonable explanation of why theism is much more believable than naturalism.

Robert Jastrow is not a Christian, but he clearly shows that the big bang theory is the "crux" of the story of Genesis in his excellent book *God and the Astronomers*. Jastrow is a world-class astronomer, yet this is an easy-to-read book.

We discovered *The Genesis Connection* by John Wiester, our science adviser, many years ago (he was way ahead of his time). It's now available from IBRI, P.O. Box 423, Hatfield, PA 19440.

◼ ◼ ◼

Questions for Reflection and Discussion

1. What was your view of the big bang before reading this chapter? What is your view now? Explain why the big bang inevitably points to God?

2. What's the difference between "simple" faith and "reasonable" faith? Why is it necessary for a maturing Christian to develop a reasonable faith?

3. Which requires more faith: believing that the universe happened by random, undirected causes, or that it was the act of an intelligent designer? Support your answer.

4. How does an expanding universe show that it began with a single big bang event?

5. Why do you think it's so difficult for many scientists to acknowledge the existence of a personal, purposeful, intelligent Creator? What else would need to happen—or what else would science have to discover—to convince the science community that such a Creator exists?

6. Explain this statement: "Naturalism offers fewer resources than theism." What does theism offer that naturalism can't possibly include?

7. Give some examples of how the evidence of design in our universe points to a personal Creator rather than an undirected, random beginning.

◻ ◻ ◻

Moving On...

We've mentioned the finely tuned universe but haven't gone into much detail. Well, in the next chapter you're going to read about some of the remarkable detail that God built into our universe so that we could live here quite comfortably.

The concept of intelligent design doesn't point to a cold, impersonal Creator who mechanically went through the motions of Creation. As you will see, the fact that our universe is so incredibly and irreducibly designed points to a Creator who is loving, caring, and personal.

Chapter 6

It seems to me that when confronted with
the marvels of life and the universe one
must ask why and not just how.

—Professor Arthur L. Schawlow,
Stanford University

We have a friend who loves to tell the story of when his son was getting ready to move away from home. Although he had lived in the dorms while at college, the son really still considered his parents' house to be his *home*. But now, after graduation, and upon securing a job in the "real world," the son was moving into a place of his own. With a fond, final look around his parents' house (with all of its furniture, food, and other accoutrements), the son asked, "Why would I want to leave all of this?" His father was quick to remark, "Because it is not yours!" To which the son replied, "But I'll never find a place to live as perfect as this." (We suspect that by "perfect" our friend's son meant "a place where someone else pays all of the bills.")

This chapter is all about living in a perfect place. We aren't talking about an exclusive housing development on a golf course in your city. We're talking about living on a planet that has conditions that are "just right" for life. After all, the other planets in our own solar system aren't very attractive alternatives (unless you don't mind being freeze-dried or having your flesh melt).

Here's the big question you need to keep in mind as we review the factual evidence for Earth's perfect conditions: Was it just the result of random, unplanned chance that Earth is perfectly suited for life, or was it part of some well-planned grand design?

Earth: A Nice Place to Call "Home"

*W*e all remember the story of Goldilocks. She was the juvenile offender who committed acts of trespass, breaking and entering, and vandalism against the Bear family. (Sorry. Bruce is a lawyer, and he required that we not trivialize her malicious acts of criminality and flagrant disregard of the law.) Anyway, the point of her story is that she was looking for something that perfectly suited her needs or desires. Whether it was a chair, or a bowl of porridge, or a bed, she only settled for what was "just right."

Imagine yourself as a cosmic Goldilocks. You are flitting around the universe looking for a planet that is "just right" for life. Some are "too cold." Some are "too hot." But planet Earth seems to be "just right." Now, is it a coincidence that Earth is perfectly suited to your needs? Are there other planets you could have chosen?

Finding a planet that is suitable for life involves much more than just its temperature. Don't forget that little thing that we like to call "air," which is required for one of your favorite activities: breathing. Actually, the list of what you will require for a comfortable existence is quite extensive. Maybe you've never realized how finicky and persnickety you are when it comes to finding a place to live. The thing is, you are not just fussy; you are also very fragile.

We think you are going to be fascinated by the information we have for you in this chapter. At least, you should be fascinated by it. It's all about you and the conditions that are necessary for your life. (After all, it might come in handy if you ever decide to leave planet Earth in search of somewhere else to live.)

A "Fine-Tuned" Universe

Scientists have determined that there are 65 or so parameters that must be "fine-tuned" if life is to exist. (We'll tell you where to find the complete list when you get to the Dig Deeper section at the end of this chapter.) If any one of these is missing, then life is impossible. Aren't you glad that our universe has the full complement? Here is a partial list to give you an idea of what we are talking about:

- *The gravitational force:* If it was stronger than it is, then the stars would be too hot, and they would burn up quickly and unevenly. If it was weaker than it is, then stars would remain so cool that nuclear fusion would never ignite (and you know the problems that would cause).

- *The ratio of the number of protons to the number of electrons:* If the ratio were either greater or smaller, then electromagnetism would dominate gravity, which would prevent the formation of stars and planets.

- *The expansion rate of the universe:* If it expanded at a faster rate, no galaxies would be able to form. If the rate were slower, then the universe would have collapsed prior to star formation.

- **The velocity of light:** If light traveled faster, the stars would be too luminous for us to tolerate. If light traveled slower, the stars would not be luminous enough.

- **The electromagnetic force:** With a force either stronger or weaker, there would be insufficient chemical bonding. (If you can't get your chemicals to bond, the whole thing falls apart.)

- **The mass density of the universe:** A greater mass density would have produced too much deuterium (a form of hydrogen) from the big bang (so stars would burn too rapidly). With smaller mass density, there would be insufficient helium from the big bang (so too few heavy elements would form).

The list goes on. For example, you couldn't live in a universe that was either too much older or too much younger. If it were older, then there would be no solar-type stars in a stable burning phase in the right part of the galaxy. If the universe were younger, then no solar-type star in a stable burning phase would have formed yet. (Apparently, our sun—a "solar-type star"—is in a stable burning phase. This is good for us, because it means that we can count on its reliability.) But in the early and late phases of solar-type stars, they burn at rates that are erratic. Maybe it's like when your dad used to barbecue with charcoal briquettes. Since he could never get the barbecue heat the same, you never knew if the steak was going to be raw or charred to a crisp. What your dad was trying to achieve was a steady burning phase of the briquettes. See, he was almost like an astrophysicist—but in a goofy barbecue apron.

And there are lots more factors in the universe that must be fine-tuned to permit life. Think about supernova eruptions for a moment. A supernova is a cataclysmic explosion of a massive star in which most of the star is blown off into interstellar space. Life would not be possible in any universe where the supernova explosions were even a little different than in our own universe:

- If the eruptions were too close or too frequent or too soon, then the radiation would exterminate life on the planet.

- If the eruptions were too far away or too infrequent or too late, then there would not be enough heavy element ashes for the formation of rocky planets.

Dr. Hugh Ross uses the term *fine-tuning* when he describes the conditions that must be present in the universe to permit life. We think this is a very accurate and descriptive term. Think of trying to find a radio station on a nondigital radio—you know, the kind that has the knob that has to be twisted to find the station you are seeking. To get the radio station to come in clearly, you have to do some "fine tuning." The dial has to be set "just right" in order for the reception to come in clearly. The tuning parameters are very narrow. If you move the dial just a little bit to the left or a little bit to the right, you'll lose the station.

The parameters for life in the universe are very narrow. For example, if the strong nuclear force were just 0.3 percent stronger or 0.2 percent weaker, the universe would never be able to support life. The expansion rate of the universe has even tighter parameters. Life couldn't be possible in a universe that had an expansion rate different than ours by more than one part out of 10^{55}. (We don't even know what to call a number that has 55 zeros. It must be something like a "bazilliongillion." So that would mean that a universe couldn't permit life if the expansion rate is off by one bazilliongillionth of a percent.)

A "So Special" Solar System

The universe isn't the only aspect of the cosmos that has to be finely tuned to permit life. Let's get a little closer to home. By "closer" we mean our own solar system.

The U.S. Declaration of Independence states that "all men are created equal." (If written in the gender-neutral terminology of the twenty-first century, that statement would read, "All people are created equal.") Well, that may be true for people, but it is not true for solar systems. At least they are not equal in terms of their capacity to support life.

You might think that our sun is just a plain ol' star like the billions of other stars in the Milky Way galaxy. Not so. Our sun has a planetary system (the "solar system"), which is made up of the nine planets (Mercury, Venus, Earth, Mars, Jupiter, Saturn, Uranus, Neptune, and Pluto). Our solar system has certain features that allow life (you are proof of that), but these features are not common to all other solar systems. Perhaps you haven't appreciated the following facts about your solar system, but without these characteristics, you wouldn't exist:

- *You need a solar system that has one, and only one, star.* It is a good thing that you only have one star (the sun) in your solar system. If you had more than one, the tidal interactions would throw your planet's orbit out of whack. This factor eliminates 60 percent of the solar systems as candidates for a place that would support life. By the way, if you had less than one star (that would be none), then you would be desperate for a heat source (and you can't live long huddled over a can of Sterno in the coldness on a sunless planet).

- *You need a star in your solar system that is the right age.* When stars are newly formed, their burning rate and temperature are not stable. They only begin to maintain a stable burning phase after they have matured a bit. If the star is too old or too young, then the luminosity of the star changes too quickly to allow life.

- *The star in your solar system has to be a certain size.* If the mass of the star is too large, then its luminosity changes too quickly and it will burn too rapidly. If the star's size is too small, then you have another set of problems: The range of distances necessary for life will be too narrow; tidal forces will knock the planet's rotational period out of sync; and there won't be enough ultraviolet radiation for plants to make sugars and oxygen. Ninety-nine percent of all stars are the wrong size for what you are looking for in a solar system.

- ***The star has to be a certain distance from the planet.*** If the star were too far away, the planet temperature would be too cool to permit a stable water evaporation cycle. If the star were too close to the planet, the climate would be too warm for a stable water cycle. If the distance from the earth to the sun differed by just 2 percent, then no plant life would be possible. This parameter eliminates 99 percent of all stars.

And a solar system that is conducive for life must have more than just a star. Don't forget about other planets. They aren't there just for decoration. They serve a very useful purpose, as planetary scientist George Wetherill of the Carnegie Institution of Washington, D.C., discovered about Jupiter:

- Jupiter is two and one-half times larger in mass than all of the other planets combined. (If you are a trivia buff, then you already know that Jupiter is about 88,500 miles in diameter, while the earth is "only" about 7900 miles in diameter. If you aren't a trivia buff, you know it now. This information may be helpful if you are ever a television game show contestant.)

- Jupiter protects the earth from getting hit by comets and other outer space debris. Its gravitational force (caused by its huge mass) either draws comets to it, or repels and deflects comets out of our solar system.

- Wetherill determined that comets would strike Earth 1000 times more frequently if it weren't for Jupiter. (Since it is believed that the extinction of the dinosaurs is due, at least in significant part, to a comet crash, we should be glad that Jupiter is hanging around.)

Wetherill said that if Jupiter weren't around, then "we wouldn't be around to study the origin of the solar system."

And our neighboring planets serve other useful purposes, too. French astrophysicist Jacques Laskar discovered that the orbits of Jupiter and Saturn keep the earth's orbit from becoming chaotic.

Without the orbital stability produced by Jupiter and Saturn, the earth's orbit would make extreme changes, causing instability in our climate and making the earth uninhabitable.

And don't forget about the moon. It serves more than a romantic purpose. The earth needs the moon's gravitational pull to produce the necessary tidal effects (which are required for cleansing coastal waters and replenishing nutrients). The moon's gravity also helps to stabilize the earth's axis tilt. By the way, just any moon wouldn't do. It takes a moon exactly the size of the one that we have (which is unique among solar systems because it is unusually large relative to the size of its planet). But if it were much larger or smaller, then the climatic and tidal disruptions on Earth would be severe.

𝒯he List Keeps Growing

This chapter is all about the characteristics of the universe, our galaxy, and our planet that have to be "just right" for life to exist. There are currently about 41 such characteristics that scientists have identified. But the list keeps growing as scientific discoveries occur and as advanced technologies make further determinations possible. In 1966, scientists knew of only two such parameters. By the end of the 1960s, the list was up to eight. The number increased to 23 by the end of the 1970s, and to 30 by the end of the 1980s. It seems that with each passing decade, science determines that the possibility for life elsewhere becomes more remote. Or, viewed another way, the earth appears to be designed particularly for our needs.

A "Just Right" Earth

Well, we looked at the parameters that must exist for life to be possible in the universe, then in our own galaxy. Now let's get really "up close and personal" and see the permissible parameters for life on our own planet. All of the following factors affect the viability of life on this planet. A change in the parameters of any one of them would either prevent the existence of life or make it extremely unpleasant:

- *The orbital pattern around the sun*—a change could produce extreme temperature changes that would make life impossible.

- *The tilt of the earth's axis*—the differential in the surface temperature would be too extreme.

- *The speed of the earth's rotation*—temperature changes and wind velocities would be too great.

- *The age of the earth*—the earth would rotate too fast (if it were much younger) or too slow (if it were much older).

- *The earth's albedo* (which, as everybody knows, is the ratio of reflected light to the total light falling on the earth's surface)—too much reflected light would cause the earth to be overwhelmed by glaciers; too little reflected light would produce a runaway greenhouse effect.

- *The ratio of oxygen to nitrogen in the earth's atmosphere*—life functions would be severely impacted by any change in this ratio.

Some factors that existed in the past are what makes life sustainable now. (When we say "past," we're talking billions of years past.) When the earth was in its young, formative stages, it rotated at a much faster rate than it does now. That rapid rotation decreased the size of the earth's weather systems and "pushed" most of them around the equator. This allowed more light and heat from the sun to penetrate the earth's atmosphere, facilitating growth of elementary life-forms.

And even some events that we would consider disasters, such as earthquakes, are actually necessary for sustaining life. Without plate movements that cause earthquakes, essential nutrients on the continents would erode into the oceans. So earthquakes are good. But there can be too much of a good thing (as anyone in California can tell you). So even earthquakes (which are scientifically referred to as "tectonic plate activity") must function within limited parameters if life is to be sustained on Earth.

And don't fail to appreciate the importance of the precise size of the earth. The mass of the earth determines its gravitational force. If the earth were much smaller, then the gravitational force wouldn't be strong enough to hold the necessary atmosphere. And if the earth were too much larger, then the gravitational force could give you an effective weight of 700 to 900 pounds (which in the disco era of the 1970s would have accelerated the tectonic plate activity).

What Are the Odds of That?

You might be wondering whether it is possible to calculate the odds of having all of the necessary parameters for life on one planet. Well, for us it isn't, but Dr. Hugh Ross has made this calculation. Not even considering about a dozen parameters which are still being studied to determine their sensitivity in the support of life (such as atmospheric transparency and greenhouse gases), Dr. Ross has analyzed 41 factors and the probability that each feature would fall within the required range. Then he calculated the probability that all of these factors would occur together so that he could estimate the possibility that a planet would exist capable of supporting life by natural means alone. Here is how he described the results of his calculation:

> Thus, with considerable security, we can draw the conclusion that much fewer than a trillionth of a trillionth of a trillionth of a trillionth of a percent of all stars could possibly possess, without divine intervention, a planet capable of sustaining advanced life (from *The Creator and the Cosmos*).

A trillionth of a trillionth of a trillionth of a trillionth of a percent. Okay, we aren't sure that we can conceptualize such a remote possibility, so allow us to refer to it as just a teeny-weeny percent of the time. Even so, we thought that with all of the stars and planets, there would probably be quite a few planets capable of supporting life (even if it was only a teeny-weeny percent of all of them). Maybe you are thinking the same thing. We hope so, because then we wouldn't be the only ones who are cosmologically challenged (which is the politically correct way to refer to someone who is an astronomical ignoramus).

Apparently, there aren't as many planets floating around in outer space as we thought. As it turns out, only nine planets have been directly *observed* in the universe. These, of course, are the planets in our own solar system. We just assumed that if our sun has nine of them, then every star has its share. Boy, were we wrong. There is evidence to suggest, however, that other planets exist. According to Dr. Ross, astronomers have been able to detect "perturbations" (small disturbances) in the positions of several stars, revealing the presence of other planet-sized bodies. Also, there are dusty disks surrounding many young stars. But only slowly rotating bachelor stars similar to the sun have the possibility of stable planets. According to Dr. Ross, the universe probably contains no more than one planet for every thousand stars. An extreme upper limit would be an average of one planet per star.

Now let's get back to the odds of finding a planet that would support life:

- The observable universe is considered to have less than a trillion galaxies, but let's round up to an even trillion to give us better odds of finding a place to live. (Scientists wouldn't quibble over using a trillion as an estimate, so we shouldn't either.)

- It would also be fair to figure that each galaxy has an average of 100 billion stars (that's 100,000,000,000).

- As we discussed in the preceding paragraph, an upper limit for the number of planets is one planet for each star. (Again, we are using the upper limit because we want the odds to be as great as possible. Hey, this is our existence we are talking about.)

- Okay, now we need to estimate the number of planets in the universe. Are you ready? Do you have fresh batteries in your calculator?

❏ One trillion galaxies (1,000,000,000,000)

❏ Times 100 billion stars per galaxy (100,000,000,000)

❏ Times 1 planet per star

❏ Equals 100 billion trillion planets (100,000,000,000,000,000,000,000)

So with 100 billion trillion planets to choose from, surely there must be many that fit within the necessary parameters for life. Even with only teeny-weeny odds in our favor, surely there would be a few likely candidates out of a pool of 100 billion trillion planets. Well, not so fast, Hubble-head. Don't go jumping to cosmological miscalculations.

Remember what *teeny-weeny* stands for: There is only a trillionth of a trillionth of a trillionth of a trillionth of one percent chance that by natural means alone there would exist a planet with the minimum 41 factors necessary for supporting life. That percentage is 10^{53}. In numerals, that percentage is 0.00000000-000000000000000000000000000000000000000001 (that is 1 with 52 zeros in front of it). With those odds, we couldn't even expect that one planet would fit the necessary criteria (because we only have 100 billion trillion available to us).

Now this is where it gets interesting. This is where you get to weigh the evidence to see if it supports the Darwinist view or the intelligent design position. Remember this: The odds are stacked heavily against any planet being suitable for life. But against the odds, all 41 of the narrow parameters for life happen to exist on one planet (the one you happen to be living on). Now think about this: How did this happen? Does planet Earth fit within the parameters for life just by chance or because our number came up in the random, undirected processes of the universe, or was intelligent design involved in creating Earth (and its galaxy and universe) so that this planet would be particularly and uniquely suited to sustain life?

𝒯ake a Shot at This Analogy

Let's say that everyone is in agreement that the odds make it extremely unlikely that life could exist anywhere in the universe except on Earth. The acknowledgment of this fact is not a concession on the part of the Darwinists. They say that it proves their point: An extremely unlikely event happened by chance. They interpret the existence of all of the necessary parameters of the earth, our solar system, and the universe as being random, undirected events that happened by chance against the odds. They say, "That's what chance is all about."

Philosopher William Lane Craig responds to the Darwinists with this analogy:

- Suppose a hundred sharpshooters are sent to execute a prisoner by firing squad. The sharpshooters all raise their rifles, aim at the prisoner, and fire.

- Suppose that the prisoner survives—that not a single bullet strikes him.

- The prisoner could conclude that, since he is alive, all of the sharpshooters missed by some extremely unlikely chance. The odds are totally against that happening, but "that's what chance is all about."

Craig reasoned that the prisoner might want to attribute his life to pure luck, but it would be far more reasonable to conclude that some intelligent designer was behind the event. Isn't it more likely to conclude that someone loaded all of the guns with blanks, or that someone persuaded all of the sharpshooters to deliberately miss? In other words, isn't it more reasonable that someone took care of the details to make sure that the prisoner lived?

Basically, you are standing in the position of the prisoner. Oh, you don't have 100 rifle barrels pointing at your chest, but you do have all of those cosmological parameters swirling around you that are a threat to your existence. (Bullets or asteroids—either way you are a sitting duck.) You have the same decision to make as that which confronted the prisoner. Is your existence a matter of luck, or was there an intelligent designer working behind the scenes to make sure that you would be able to live?

"What's That Again?"

1. Life can't happen everywhere. In fact, life couldn't exist anywhere within our entire universe if it weren't for certain factors that exist and are constant. Scientists have identified at least 25 of these parameters. If any one of them were off, some by the tiniest fraction, then life wouldn't be possible. The universe is finely tuned for life.

2. The same can be said for our solar system. Life couldn't exist on Earth if any one of a number of factors were slightly different. Everything has to be in its place. If Jupiter were much smaller, for example, we would probably have suffered the same fate as the dinosaurs.

3. Many of the features of Earth itself are "just right" for life. You couldn't live here if any one of certain parameters were a bit different. From the tilt of the earth, to the ratio of oxygen to nitrogen in the atmosphere, all of the factors have to be present or you wouldn't be.

4. The odds are astronomical (pun intended) against any planet existing that has all of the parameters necessary for life. There is only a trillionth of a trillionth of a trillionth of a trillionth of one percent chance that by natural means alone there would exist a planet with the minimum 41 factors necessary for supporting life.

Dig Deeper

In writing this chapter, we relied heavily upon *The Creator and the Cosmos* by Hugh Ross, Ph.D. Don't be intimidated by Dr. Ross's brain. It must be huge, but the book is understandable even if you don't have a hobby that involves a telescope. Make sure that you get an updated version of the book because the first edition has been revised to include recent scientific discoveries that Dr. Ross believes strengthen the evidence for creation by God.

Another Hugh Ross book, maybe a bit less technical, is *The Fingerprint of God*. In this book, Dr. Ross reviews some basic scientific principles of cosmology, and then examines what the Bible says about cosmological matters.

The Creation Hypothesis (J. P. Moreland, editor) is filled with "scientific evidence for an Intelligent Designer." That's actually the subtitle of the book. Check out chapter 8 ("Astronomical Evidences for a Personal Transcendent God" by Dr. Hugh Ross) for the lists of design parameters in our universe, galaxy, and earth that must be present for life to exist.

▫ ▫ ▫

*Q*uestions for *R*eflection and *D*iscussion

1. Explain the principle of "fine tuning" in the origins debate. How does this principle fit into the consideration of whether the universe was created for our existence (intelligent design theory) or merely happened by random chance (Darwinism)?

2. What are some of the "fine tuning" parameters that must exist in the universe if you are to remain alive?

3. Perhaps you took our solar system for granted before you read this chapter. What are some of the features of our solar system that you now appreciate?

4. The earth is "just right" for human life. What factors, if changed just a little bit, would make our planet uninhabitable?

5. Here is a homework assignment. Find out what would be the odds of winning a state lottery. How do those odds compare to "a trillionth of a trillionth of a trillionth of a trillionth of a percent?" How many zeros would you need to see before you would consider that the odds for all factors existing in the universe, solar system, and Earth are too remote to occur without an intelligent designer behind it all?

6. Explain how this quote applies to the consideration of whether our universe was designed or happened by random processes: "Things don't happen by chance. *Chance* is not a force. It just describes the odds of whether or not something will happen."

7. How does William Lane Craig's "firing squad" analogy explain the contrast between assuming "luck" versus an intelligent, intervening cause?

Moving On...

Okay, we found you a place to live. It wasn't easy. We had to look at a hundred billion trillion planets, but we finally found one. So you've got a place to live, but there is no life on it yet. That comes in the next chapter.

There is evidence that life existed on Earth as long as 3.5 billion years ago. Now when we say "life," we aren't talking about civilizations with malls and minimarts. We are talking about single-celled organisms. But that is all life was 3.5 billion years ago.

The interesting question in the next chapter is, How did life progress from cells to animals? (We are saving the discussion of human life for chapter 8. You are so special that you deserve a chapter all your own.) We hope you aren't allergic to fossil dust.

Chapter 7

I myself am convinced that the theory of
evolution, especially to the extent to which
it has been applied, will be one of the
greatest jokes in the history books of the
future. Posterity will marvel that so very
flimsy and dubious a hypothesis could be
accepted with the incredible credulity it has.

—*Malcolm Muggeridge*

What do we know so far from chapters 5 and 6? (Don't worry. That question was rhetorical. We wouldn't put you on the spot without warning.) We've got a universe that was big banged into existence. And we have a planet that is situated in that universe in such a way that it is "just right" for life. There's only one problem. We don't have *life* yet. But don't worry. You are only a page away. Well, actually, you (human life) are an entire chapter away. We won't talk about you until chapter 8. But we'll start talking about actual life of the plant and animal variety on the next page.

The origin of life is a very hot topic in the debate between Darwinism and intelligent design. How did life get started on Earth? Your conclusions about the beginnings of plant and animal life will strongly influence your opinions about how human life began. So don't think that you can skip this chapter just because you are anxious to read chapter 8 for confirmation that your uncle is a Neanderthal.

Maybe botany and zoology weren't your favorite subjects in school (nor ours either), but that's because the term paper on soil erosion was boring, and the classification of bird beaks seemed irrelevant to real life. But in this chapter, there's lots of adventure ahead, and it is all relevant to life because it's all about how life began.

So grab your paleontologist's shovel and your Indiana Jones hat. We've got lots of digging to do. We have to work down through the fossil record about 65 million years deep until we hit evidence of the dinosaurs. We'll have to go even deeper than that if we want to wade in the prebiotic swamps when all of life was just a bunch of single-cell organisms. (In case we forget to tell you when we get there, don't drink the water.)

The Origin of Life: Fossils and Cells Have a Lot to Tell

What's Ahead

- ☐ Three Possible Explanations for the Start of It All

- ☐ Prebiotic Soup—Is It Hard to Swallow?

- ☐ How Life Moved Along—Theory, Facts, and Fossils

- ☐ Cambrian Explosion—Too Many Too Quickly

- ☐ Irreducible Complexity—It Can't Get More Basic Than This

A major fundamental principle of science is observation. You perform an experiment, and you observe what happens. Well, science has a real challenge when it comes to the origin of life—there was no one around to observe how it started. No one was hiding in the bushes to sneak a peek at whether God created life or whether it spontaneously occurred. (That's because no person existed at that point, and neither did bushes.)

So what is science to do about determining how life came to planet Earth? Well, we still fall back on observation, but we have to observe clues in the present world upon which we can base our theories and explanations.

In this chapter, we're going to look at some theories for how life began and how it progressed. The scientific community is fairly well agreed on *when* life-forms began, but there is sure a difference of opinion as to how life came into existence.

What Did the First Life-Form Look Like?

Before you start looking for how life began, maybe we ought to tell you what it looked like.

There appears to be a broad consensus among scientists that the first life appeared on Earth about 3.86 billion years ago. That was when the first "cyanobacteria" appeared. This was a very primitive, algae-like life-form. Life-forms didn't progress very quickly at the start. After about one billion years, the earth still wasn't home to much more than mounds of cyanobacteria (called "stromatolites") that flourished and accumulated in the shallow-water seas.

If you were expecting the first life-forms to be animals, you would be off by about three billion years. The first organisms with skeletons (coral and shellfish) didn't appear until about 530 million years ago during the Cambrian period of the Paleozoic era. If you're anxious to jump ahead, we won't make you wait another couple billion years. We talk about the "Cambrian Explosion" later in this chapter.

Three Possible Explanations for the Start of It All

There are many explanations for how life began on Earth. Scientists aren't the only folks who have an opinion on this subject. A lot of kooks do, too. However, we're going to stick to the three primary scientific explanations that seem the most probable. (We are arbitrarily omitting any explanation that attributes the beginning of life to Elvis or to a conspiracy involving President Kennedy's assassination.)

Try one of these three on for size.

Explanation #1 for the Beginning of Life: God

Maybe God did it. Or if you don't want to give Him a name, then an intelligent designer. This explanation asserts that there was an outside power or agent that initiated or guided the initiation of life on Earth. The proponents of this view emphasize that origin-of-life experiments have failed to show that natural processes are capable of creating life.

We will examine the evidence that supports this intelligent-design theory a little later in the chapter. Evidence of intelligent design is not limited to life-forms as simple as bacteria and blue-green algae. As we will discuss later in this chapter, there is evidence of an outside "creator" even with reptiles, birds, and mammals. If you are persuaded by the intelligent design theory for the creation of an ostrich, a camel, and a rhinoceros, then you shouldn't have any trouble applying the theory to the first bacteria.

Explanation #2 for the Beginning of Life: It Came from Outer Space

Maybe life came from outer space. Perhaps there is life in some other part of the universe and some spore-like life-form traveled into our atmosphere. This is possible, though not very probable. Space travel, even for tiny bacteria, can be pretty rough. There are few life-forms that could withstand the radiation and extreme heat and cold that would be encountered in travel between the planets. And the distances involved make this possibility even more remote. It is not likely that a planet orbiting a star would intercept a spore released from the atmosphere on another planet near another star.

Even if this theory is correct, it doesn't solve our problem of determining how life began. It just shifts the inquiry from our planet to another one. The question would still remain: "How did life on (insert planet name here) begin?"

There has been much research (and a lot of tax dollars) devoted to finding life in outer space. So far, nothing determinative has been found. And considering the odds against life existing elsewhere in the universe—as we discussed in chapter 6—

it seems unlikely that life originated elsewhere and came to earth. In fact, if anything, it seems more likely it would have occurred the other way around. There is some speculation that spore-like bacteria from earth may have traveled to other planets (after all, we have all of that spacecraft debris and astronaut litter floating around in outer space). Now let's move to the third explanation, one that is at the heart of Darwinism.

Explanation #3 for the Beginning of Life: It Just Happened by Itself

Darwinists promote the explanation that life (in the form of the first living cell) developed from nonliving matter under certain chemical conditions. This explanation is referred to as *prebiotic evolution*. (*Prebiotic* means "before biological life.") This theory proposes that matter and energy and atmospheric conditions on Earth 3.5 billion years ago interfaced in such a way as to bring complex life-forms (cells) into existence. This theory acknowledges that finding the right combination of matter and the necessary conditions to produce life probably didn't happen at first, but instead required billions of years until the right one clicked.

With Darwinism as the prevailing scientific theory for the origin and development of life, Explanation #3 is the one most universally held. For that reason, let's take a closer look at it.

Prebiotic Soup—Is It Hard to Swallow?

The Darwinist position for the origin of life is that it came from a chance combination of nonliving chemicals. For hundreds of years, people believed that some life-forms could originate suddenly, without any predecessor life-forms to produce them. This was the concept of *spontaneous generation*. Don't be too critical of your ancestors who believed this theory. They were just using the scientific principle of observation (although their observations were too limited and their interpretations were incorrect). But how could you blame them, when you consider the following:

If a piece of meat were left to decay on the floor, pretty soon it would be covered by maggots. The maggots didn't parade into the room from the front door marching in a line to the meat. They just appeared on the meat. Where did they come from? You can understand how it is possible that some people believed that certain types of life-forms arose "spontaneously," without any preexisting life to produce them. (Plus this belief probably served as good motivation to keep people from leaving rotting meat on the floor.)

The theory of spontaneous generation was accepted before the invention of the microscope because no one was able to observe the bacteria on the meat. Once bacteria could be observed, then the theory started to fall apart. In 1688, Francesco Redi performed experiments with rotting meat and maggots which raised serious doubts about the theory of spontaneous generation. Although Redi disproved the spontaneous generation of large (macroscopic) organisms with his "no maggots from nothing" experiments, the question still remained whether a bacterium could form by itself. Even when experiments were done using a "sterile" flask, bacteria would seemingly appear out of nowhere and nothing. If the spontaneous generation of bacteria was possible, then the origin of life could be explained by that theory.

In the 1860s, Louis Pasteur demonstrated that the growth of bacteria in a supposedly "sterile" environment was not spontaneous generation of bacteria at all. He proved that airborne, live microbial spores contaminated the flasks. It wasn't a sterile environment.

The research begun by Pasteur was further supported by about a century of scientific exploration and better understanding of the complexity of cells. By the early part of the twentieth century, it was the universally recognized conclusion that life comes only from preexisting life. Almost every scientist now believes that cells can only come from other cells.

Prebiotic Soup for the Ailing Darwinists

Refuting the theory of spontaneous generation of cells didn't discourage the Darwinists. While they admit that spontaneous generation of cells is not possible now, they theorize that it was possible at least 3.5 billion years ago, when conditions on Earth's surface and in its atmosphere were different. In other words, *it couldn't happen now, but it did happen back then.*

As support for their theory of spontaneous generation of the first cells, Darwinists rely on the following:

- In 1924, a Russian biochemist, A. I. Oparin, theorized that the atmosphere of the early earth was completely different than it is now. He speculated that energy sources (from volcanic heat or lightning) acted on simple carbon compounds in the atmosphere, transforming them into more complicated compounds. These compounds came together in the oceans to form the microscopic clumps that were the predecessors to the first cells.

In the 1970s Harvard professor Elso Barghoorn, a paleontologist, discovered microfossils of bacteria and algae in rocks close to 3.5 billion years old.

- A similar theory was promoted in 1928 by an English biochemist, J. B. S. Haldane. He hypothesized that the sun's ultraviolet light caused the simple gases in the atmosphere (carbon dioxide, methane, water vapor, and ammonia) to transform into organic compounds, turning the primitive ocean into a hot "soup." From this "soup" came virus-like particles that turned into the first cells.

- In the 1950s, the Oparin-Haldane hypothesis was "tested" by a graduate student at the University of Chicago, Stanley Miller, and his professor, Harold Urey (who won the 1934 Nobel prize in Chemistry). Miller and Urey designed an apparatus that attempted to duplicate the atmospheric conditions of primitive earth which are the basis for the Oparin-Haldane hypothesis. The Miller-Urey experiments didn't produce cells, but they did result in the production of several amino acids that are the building blocks of proteins.

But This Soup Recipe Doesn't Cook

Darwinists place great reliance on the "simulation" experiments of Miller-Urey. Without a doubt, the results are fascinating. However, the experiments only supported the first phase of the Oparin-Haldane hypothesis. They didn't reach the next step of moving toward cellular formation. And there are considerable problems with the Miller-Urey experiments (and the underlying assumptions) which make them far less reliable than many Darwinists want to admit.

- **The Oxygen Problem.** The Oparin-Haldane hypothesis assumes that there was no oxygen in the atmosphere of primitive earth. Thus, Miller and Urey eliminated any trace of oxygen from their experiments. (By the way, eliminating oxygen was a good idea, because if it had been included here, it would have blown up the experiment.)

But this assumption may be fatally flawed. The present volume of the earth's atmosphere is 21 percent oxygen. If the oxygen level in the atmosphere of early earth had been only 1 percent, then it would have been impossible for organic compounds to form. Recent geological discoveries have indicated that significant amounts of oxygen may have been present about 3.5 billion years ago. While these new findings are not conclusive, they put the Oparin-Haldane assumption of an oxygen-free atmosphere into serious doubt.

- **The Problem of Realistic Starting Materials.** Scientists now believe that methane and ammonia were not present in the early atmosphere. Removal of these gases and their replacement by the correct early gases (water vapor, carbon dioxide, and nitrogen) yields few, if any, amino acids.

- **The Problem of Reversible Reactions.** The Oparin-Haldane assumptions rely on energy to bring the cells together. But here is the paradox: The energy required to drive (some, but not all) reactions forward is even more likely to break them apart. This is especially true of more complex molecules that would quickly break down to simple compounds. For this reason, the Miller-Urey apparatus includes a trap to catch the organic compounds before they can be exposed to energy. (Some have suggested that this is like cheating on a test!)

- *The Problem of Cross-Reactions.* Amino acids, rather than combining with each other, are more likely to combine with other ingredients in the prebiotic soup, thus ending their potential to become useful protein molecules. (In the actual experiments, the predominant outcome was larger yields of nonbiological goo.)

- *The Problem of Equal Mixtures.* Amino acids come in two forms. They are classified as either L-forms (cutely referred to as "left-handed") or D-forms (called "right-handed" for some unexplainable reason). The Oparin-Haldane hypothesis is based on the assumption that only left-handed amino acids combined to produce the proteins of life. But the Miller-Urey experiments always produced a mixture that was 50 percent left-handed amino acids and 50 percent right-handed amino acids.

There are numerous problems with the Miller-Urey experiments, but Darwinists rely on them anyway to support their belief that life on Earth began in some kind of spontaneous way in the prebiotic soup. But this soup smells a little too funny to us to swallow. Oh sure, it may be worth a few sips, but we don't think that the recipe is so "mmmmmm, good" that other possibilities (such as intelligent design) must be completely removed from the dining table of scientific inquiry. (Wow! We sure pushed that analogy for all it was worth.)

How Life Moved Along—Theory, Facts, and Fossils

Let's not spend all of our time wading knee-deep in the prebiotic soup. (After a few billion years, our skin will get wrinkly.) Let's shift our focus from how life began on Earth to how that life progressed. In other words, life started 3.5 billion years ago with just algae, but now we've got aardvarks, alligators, and anteaters. How did that all happen?

Darwinism stands for the proposition that all present life-forms descended from a single ancestor. In other words, all creatures are connected in a biological chain. Darwin considered the random, undirected acts of nature to be the breeding incubator of new species. New life-forms were the results of minor changes over many years. (Natural selection—"survival of the fittest"—caused new, useful traits to be passed on to the next generation while harmful traits were eliminated.) Given enough time, the better-equipped organism might bear little or no resemblance to its own ancestors.

Darwin recognized that if his theory was true, then the fossil record should show lots of gradual changes. He believed that the fossil record should also show gradual changes of one form changing into another one. But Darwin (and his theory) ran into one big problem: The fossil record didn't show gradual changes from one type to another. Darwin admitted this problem himself in his *On the Origin of Species:*

> The number of intermediate varieties, which have formerly existed on the earth, [must] be truly enormous. Why then is not every geological formation and every stratum full of such intermediate links? Geology assuredly does not reveal any such finely graded organic chain; and this, perhaps, is the most obvious and gravest objection which can be urged against my theory.

In fairness to Darwin, the fossil evidence wasn't very well established back in 1859 when he wrote *On the Origin of Species*. And the science of paleontology (the branch of geology that deals with prehistoric forms of life by studying plant and animal fossils) was still in its infancy. But Darwin was confident that better fossil-finding techniques in the future would vindicate his theory by revealing "transitional" fossils.

Cambrian Explosion—Too Many Too Quickly

About 120 years have passed since Darwin himself became a fossil candidate (no disrespect intended). In that time, the science of paleontology has developed and become much more sophisticated, just as Darwin had hoped. And there have been tremendous fossil discoveries, just as Darwin had hoped. But the fossil evidence we have collected in the last decade or so has pretty much undercut the foundation of Darwin's theory of gradual macroevolution.

Perhaps the greatest fossil evidence *against* Darwinism comes from the Cambrian period at the beginning of the Paleozoic era:

- Paleontologists have determined that an "explosion" of life happened around 540 million years ago. (Prior to that time, the fossil record shows pretty much just algae and some primitive ferns and other plants.)

- The beginning of the Cambrian period marked the appearance of many of the major phyla that characterize modern animal life. Over a period of only a few million years, about 70 different phyla appeared.

- The burst of multicellular life at the start of the Cambrian period was so dramatic that the *New York Times* reported this discovery under a page-wide headline on April 23, 1991: "Spectacular Fossils Record Early Riot of Creation." (We find it interesting that the *Times* used the word *Creation*. Maybe that was the only conclusion to be drawn from the fact that so many different phyla of animals appeared all at once in the fossil record.)

- Because of the abrupt appearance of almost every animal phylum, researchers refer to this phenomenon as "the Cambrian explosion." Scientists consider it to be the biological big bang.

- The evidence further shows a top-down pattern wherein the major themes of life's history (animal body designs) appear first, followed by variations on these themes (like a musical symphony). This is the opposite of the bottom-up Darwinian model, where gradual changes among lower forms are supposed to give rise to new major designs.

A phylum is the broadest classification of animals. For example, the phylum that contains human beings also includes giraffes, lizards, and parrots (basically, every animal with a backbone). If the differences within a phylum are great, then the differences between two phyla are even greater. (As much as a squirrel differs from a fish, it differs even more from a sea urchin because these differing phyla have entirely different architectural themes.)

The Cambrian explosion is a pain in the fossil for Darwinists. It doesn't reveal just a handful of species appearing at the same time. Instead, it reveals the sudden appearance of all basic designs of body architecture, so distinct that they have to be categorized in different phyla. A leading Darwinist, Richard Dawkins, conceded the obvious when he admitted that the Cambrian explosion contradicts Darwin's theory of gradual, intermediate transitional life forms: "It is as though they were just planted there, without any evolutionary history."

And the fossil record after the Cambrian period doesn't help the Darwinist much either. After the Cambrian explosion, almost no new phyla appear in the fossil record. That means there has been no new minor phylum for the last half a billion years.

The known fossil record fails to document a single example of phyletic (gradual) evolution accomplishing a major morphologic transition and hence offers no evidence that the gradualistic model can be valid.

—paleontologist Steven M. Stanley of Johns Hopkins University, from his book *Macroevolution*

The Cambrian period and all post-Cambrian periods reveal a general pattern of fossil evidence against Darwinism. Life's history reveals a pattern of the sudden appearance of novel designs rather than the accumulation of minor variations leading to these major innovations.

A Tree or a Bar Code

Two diagrams can illustrate the misconception of Darwinism, contrasted with the actual fossil record. In each of the following two pictures, the vertical axis represents the passage of time (from the bottom to the top); and the horizontal axis represents the spread of variation in animal morphology (form, shape, and structure).

According to Darwin's theory, the diagram should look like a tree. If a common ancestor relates all living things to each other, then there should be a beginning "stem" off of which all new forms will branch. There should be a multitude of transitional and intermediate forms as new novel types. Graphically depicted, Darwin's theory would look something like this:

Darwinian Predictions

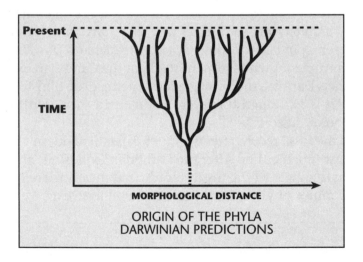

ORIGIN OF THE PHYLA
DARWINIAN PREDICTIONS

But that isn't what the fossil record reveals. First of all, there appears to be no central, beginning "stem" from which all organisms branched off. Second, few, if any, transitional or intermediate life-forms have been found. Third, the groups didn't get more diverse. (The number of new phyla has declined over time.) The graphic depiction of the actual fossil record is not a tree; instead, it looks like a bar code on a package at the grocery store:

The Fossil Evidence

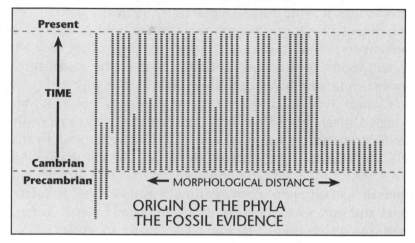

ORIGIN OF THE PHYLA
THE FOSSIL EVIDENCE

Irreducible Complexity—It Can't Get More Basic Than This

The problem of the fossil record has been tough enough for Darwinists, but they now must also face the challenge of "irreducible complexity." By definition, an "irreducibly complex system" is one that cannot be produced directly by gradual, successive modifications or refinements. In other words, it is as basic as it can get, and anything less doesn't cut it. In a biological context, an irreducibly complex system cannot be produced gradually; it would have to arise as a completed unit or it couldn't exist in the first place.

Darwin himself recognized that his theory of gradual evolution by natural selection would be fatally flawed if there were a complex organism that couldn't have been assembled in slight, successive stages. As he admitted in *On the Origin of Species:* "If it could be demonstrated that any complex organ existed which could not possibly have been formed by numerous, successive, slight modifications, my theory would absolutely break down." In other words, Darwin conceded that his theory would be invalid if there could be found an organism that was irreducibly complex.

Darwinism Caught in Behe's Mousetrap

Back in the mid to late 1800s, Darwin didn't understand the complexities of living things. At that time, before the advent of electron microscopes and advanced research techniques, the cell was thought to be nothing more than a tiny blob of gel. But what Darwin didn't understand back then is now the evidence that makes this theory "absolutely break down."

Michael Behe is a biochemist of international renown at Lehigh University. He has been the scientist most responsible for illustrating the irreducible complexity of cells. No longer are cells considered to be little blobs of gel. He emphasizes that "even the simplest self-replicating cell has the capacity to produce thousands of different proteins and other molecules, at different times and under variable conditions. Synthesis, repair, communication—all of these functions take place in virtually every cell." Not only is every cell irreducibly complex, but many of the systems within the cell are irreducibly complex in themselves.

In his bestselling book *Darwin's Black Box,* Behe uses the analogy of a simple mousetrap to illustrate the principal of irreducible complexity (which is an analogy for which our simple minds are grateful). He explains that the mousetrap consists of five parts: a platform, the holding bar, the hammer, the catch, and the spring. It doesn't work unless every part is in place. At any stage of partial assembly, the mousetrap won't function (it won't trap a mouse), because all of the components must be present for it to work.

The same thing is true of a living cell. Many of its systems won't function unless all of the parts are present. They are irreducibly complex. Because they can't get any simpler, Behe states that the Darwinists can't explain how cells arose: "Now the thing about irreducibly complex systems is that they cannot be produced by numerous small steps, because one does not acquire the function until close to the end, or at the end. Therefore, with irreducibly complex systems, they cannot be produced by Darwinian evolution."

You might be wondering how the Darwinist scientific community handles this notion of irreducible complexity. It doesn't. Behe tried to find explanations by Darwinists for how a cell might have evolved, but he came up empty-handed: "If you look in the professional science literature about how such systems arose, it turns out that nobody has published anything. Scientists simply assumed that it happened through evolution. But if you try to call them on it they can't produce anything. They just kind of wave their hands."

At life's most fundamental level—the cell—Darwinists have no explanation for how such a complex structure might have evolved.

---

*T*he Eyes Have It

If you are interested in studying a more complex example of irreducible complexity, consider the human eye. In Darwin's day, scientists knew how complicated the eye was, and they knew that each of its complex features—as well as all the complicated chemicals involved— depended on each other in order for the entire eye to function. As Behe observed, Darwin "realized that if in one generation an organ as complex as the eye suddenly appeared, it would be a miracle." Yet there wasn't then, and there isn't now, a reasonable alternative explanation.

In effect, the human eye is an "irreducibly complex biological system." No part of the eye can function unless all the other parts are already working. According to Behe, such a thing is a "powerful challenge to Darwinian evolution," because such a system cannot be produced gradually.

Puncturing Darwin's Equilibrium

Some present-day Darwinists have an explanation for why the fossil record appears to have "gaps" that defeat their theory of gradual cumulative change. Stephen Jay Gould of Harvard University and Niles Eldridge of the American Museum of Natural History have proposed a theory of "punctuated equilibrium" to explain the gaps between the different fossil groups which lack transitional, intermediate forms. Under this theory, a species remains stable for a long period of time. Then, at some point, a small population of the species becomes isolated from the rest (perhaps geographically separated). Within that small population, a rapid evolutionary change occurs (perhaps adapting to the different environmental conditions). Since the transitional population is isolated and small, it wouldn't have much chance of leaving a fossil record. Only after the "changed" population increases in number and invades and replaces the parent population will they show up as fossils. By this time, the organism appears to be completely different from its original group.

Punctuated equilibrium is a description, not an explanation. The model of punctuated equilibrium has made a major concession to the scientific record in that it accurately describes the pattern in the fossil record as being one of sudden appearance and stasis (stability). It fails, however, as an explanation for those missing transitional forms because it is based on the absence of evidence rather than on actual fossil evidence.

But Haven't Some "Missing Links" Been Found?

If the theory of Darwinism is correct then you would expect to find many "transitional" life-forms as one species "evolves" into another. Darwinists have touted several fossils as being proof that transitional forms exist. On further examination, however, the touting was premature.

> **Archaeopteryx.** First discovered in 1861, eight specimens of Archaeopteryx have appeared in the fossil record from the Jurassic period. Darwinists cited it as an example of the "transitional" evolutionary step from lizards to birds. It had wings and feathers but also had teeth (unlike any modern bird), a long lizard-like tail, and claws on its wings. But a *combination* of features doesn't necessarily mean it was transitional. The combination of structures could be "intermediate" without the creature being transitional. (Consider the duck-billed platypus. Although it has a bill like a duck and fur like a mammal, it has never been considered as a transitional life-form by evolutionists.) Paleontologists, including Darwinists, now agree that there are

too many structural differences for Archaeopteryx to be the ancestor of modern birds.

Bambiraptor. This fossil, found in Montana in 1993, was about the size of a chicken, with sharp teeth and claws, and a long tail (resembling the Velociraptor of "Jurassic Park" fame). The "real-life" drawings and models of Bambiraptor show hair-like projections on the body and feathers on the forelimbs. It was proclaimed to be the "remarkable missing link between birds and dinosaurs." But nothing remotely resembling feathers was found with the fossil. The hair-like projections and feathers are imaginary. The reconstructions gave Bambiraptor "scruffy" feathers and made it as bird-like as possible because the artist assumed its position between dinosaurs and birds. One leading ornithologist has predicted that the whole dino-bird theory will turn out to be "the greatest embarrassment of paleontology of the 20th century."

Archaeoraptor. This fossil was purchased for $80,000 at an Arizona mineral show and was heralded as "the missing link between terrestrial dinosaurs and birds that could actually fly." The fossil, supposedly smuggled out of China, had the forelimbs of a primitive bird and the tail of a dinosaur. It was the feature story in the November 1999 *National Geographic* magazine. It turns out that Archaeoraptor had the transitional features that Darwinists were looking for because a clever forger had fabricated it that way (knowing it would bring big bucks in the fossil market). Chinese paleontologist Xu Xing proved that the specimen consisted of a dinosaur tail glued to the body of a primitive bird. *National Geographic* printed a retraction.

"What's That Again?"

1. The three probable explanations for the origin of life are: a) some form of bacteria floated in from outer space, or b) it arose by the random confluence of matter and energy in a simmering prebiotic soup, or c) an intelligent designer created it. The probability of the origin of life from outer space is not seriously considered, so the explanation is likely to be either prebiotic evolution or intelligent design.

2. The assumptions of the Oparin-Haldane hypothesis for prebiotic soup are questionable (such as the absence of oxygen in the atmosphere). The Miller-Urey experiments that supposedly confirmed some of the Oparin-Haldane assumptions are also questionable (such as producing equal amounts of L-amino acids and D-amino acids, when the Oparin-Haldane hypothesis assumes only L-amino acids will result). Thus, the prebiotic evolution theory has not been proven. It remains simply that—a theory.

3. Darwin admitted that his theory of macroevolution would fail if the fossil record doesn't show gradual, transitional life-forms between species. The fossil record doesn't reveal transitional forms. Just the opposite result is revealed in the fossil record. The Cambrian explosion shows the sudden appearance of almost every animal phylum.

4. Darwin admitted that his theory would break down if organisms existed that couldn't be broken down. The current status of cellular research reveals that cells and many systems within the cells are irreducibly complex. As such, the cell cannot be produced by Darwinian evolution.

Dig Deeper

On the subject of biological origins, we recommend *Of Pandas and People*. During its developmental stages, this book was used in a public school district. It presents the theories and criticisms of current Darwinist viewpoints.

Although it is a bit on the lofty side, you might enjoy reading Michael Denton's *Evolution: A Theory in Crisis*. Denton, a physician and molecular biologist, presents recent scientific developments that challenge traditional Darwinism.

We already told you about this book: *Darwin's Black Box* by Michael J. Behe. It stands as one of the leading challenges to Darwinism.

A brand new and excellent book is *Icons of Evolution* by Jonathan Wells. This book exposes how the *theory* of evolution has been fraudently presented as *fact*.

Just for fun (after you have popped a vessel in your cranium from reading our other highly technical recommendations), pick up a copy of *What's Darwin Got to Do with It?* by Dr. Hugh Ross and Rick Bundschuh. It is a distillation of the debate over origins in comic-book form.

◻ ◼ ◻

*Q*uestions for *R*eflection and *D*iscussion

1. What are the three possibilities for how life got started on our planet? Which one seems most likely to you?

2. What is the concept of *spontaneous generation?* Can you think of any example of this theory actually existing in real life?

3. How does the graphic illustration of a "tree" exhibit Darwin's theory of what would be found in the fossil record?

4. How come the fossil evidence, when graphed in terms of time and changes, looks more like a bar code than a tree?

5. Why does the fossil evidence of the Cambrian explosion blow apart Darwin's theory?

6. What is the theory of *irreducible complexity?* How does it apply to Darwin's theory of the development of life?

7. Use the example of a mousetrap to illustrate the principle of irreducible complexity.

□ □ □

Moving On...

Well, we haven't yet completed our discussion of the origin of all life-forms. Did you notice what was missing? It was you. We stopped short of discussing the origin of the human race. Hey, even though we don't know you very well, it seems to us that you are special enough to merit your own chapter.

Actually, as we move into the next chapter, the controversy over Darwinian macroevolution will continue. In fact, it will even intensify a bit. We'll be examining the evidence for whether you are a descendant of the hominids (Neanderthal and the rest of that slump-shouldered bunch). So as you turn the page, sit up straight. You wouldn't want poor posture to reflect negatively on your ancestry.

Chapter 8

The material universe is both an essential display of the greatness and goodness of God and the arena of the eternal life of finite spirits, including the human.

—*Dallas Willard*

The prevailing scientific viewpoint of our culture is that humans descended from monkeys and apes, which in turn descended from reptiles and fish and so on. If you don't believe that, then the only other option you are left with is to believe the Bible's story of Creation, which scientists won't even dignify by calling it a "theory." In fact, the Creation account isn't taught in most public classrooms, so the only place you're going to hear about God creating the universe—and everything in it—is at home or at church.

In this chapter we want to offer you a better way of thinking. We don't want you to feel trapped between two options that seem completely incompatible. You can believe the Bible *because it's true,* and you can believe the scientific evidence *as long as it's true.*

We also want you to know that you are very important to God—so important that He created you uniquely and very specially. There is no race like the human race, and there is no individual human like you. God created you for a purpose and, as you're going to see, it's the greatest purpose in the world.

Human Life:
How We All Began

School classrooms are famous for their charts. There's the chart showing all the presidents, the chart with the flags of nations, and the periodic chart of the chemical elements (didn't you love that one?). There's the chart of the solar system, the flower chart, and the ever-present grade chart (written in code, of course).

You've seen them all, but there's one you probably remember above all others because of what it told you about yourself. It was the chart showing the "emergence of man" from a primitive monkey to a modern human. You may have seen the illustrated chart Time-Life Books published in 1972. On the left side was a scrawny primate on all fours who didn't resemble any human you had ever seen (except for your cousin Willard, but that was an entirely different matter). As you moved to the right, however, the lineup of monkeys and apes began to look more and more "human," until you got to the fully erect *Homo sapiens* on the far right (who looked a lot like your shop teacher, Mr. Cooper).

How did that chart make you feel? If you grew up believing that Darwinism was true, then you probably saw that chart as a factual presentation of the emergence of man from primates (Darwin used the phrase "descent of man" to describe the process because he believed that all life-forms descended from other life-forms).

On the other hand, if you grew up believing that God created the heavens and the earth and everything on the earth, then it's likely you saw the chart as a total misrepresentation of the story of Creation as told in the Bible. Despite your disagreement, you couldn't say anything about it to your teacher or your friends, because ever since you can remember, Darwinism has been taught as fact. As far as your school was concerned, Darwin was science, and belief in God was religion. And the two just didn't go together.

And it doesn't stop with the textbooks you read in school. All encyclopedias, the popular science books, documentaries, and media productions—virtually any place where you would go to find out about human life and how we all began—are written from the assumption that we are descended from monkeys and apes.

This line of reasoning is called an *a priori* assumption. In other words, it's accepted as fact even before you study the evidence.

The Darwin Dilemma

Now this is a rather big problem, wouldn't you agree? If Darwinism remains as the prevailing belief system of our culture, then you are left with only two options when it comes to the origin of the universe and human life:

Option #1:   Believe what the Bible says—even though it doesn't provide scientific explanations—because you believe in God.

Option #2:   Believe in science—even though it leaves God out of the picture—because it presents the alleged facts about human origins.

Now here's the problem. If you choose Option #1, you've got to throw science out the window, and if you choose Option #2, you've got to throw God out the window. And that's where most people are, whether they believe in God or not. They believe they have to hang onto their belief system without giving in to the other side, so you've got this war of words going on. You know, "Darwinists are evil," or "Christians are stupid."

There's even a war of *symbols* that we find downright ridiculous. Have you seen this little battle of the bumper stickers? First there was the fish sticker, symbolizing belief in God. Then some joker, obviously a Darwinist, came up with an irritating response: a fish with little feet and the word *DARWIN* printed inside. Not to be outdone, some enterprising fish-symbol advocate designed a Darwin fish being "eaten" by a larger fish symbol.

What's next? A symbol showing Darwin devouring God? There may be some truth (and more than a little amusement) in all of this bumper-sticker madness, but it's not doing anybody any good. The search for truth, especially the truth about the origin and purpose of the human race, isn't going to be settled by one side beating up the other. It isn't a matter of choosing what the Bible says or choosing what science says. There is a better way to think.

If you're bogged down by these two options (or worse, you find yourself floundering between the two), we've got good news for you. When it comes to science and the Bible and how we humans got here in the first place, there is a better option.

Option #3: You can believe the Bible—because it's true. And you can believe science—as long as it's true.

At the end of chapter 3 we defined the key terminology that frames the debate between Darwinism and intelligent design. Let's group these terms into each of the first two options:

The Bible

- *Creationism*—This is the belief that God created the universe and everything in it. Young earth creationism believes the Creation process began about 10,000 years ago and took six literal 24-hour days. Old earth creationism believes the universe is billions of years old because the "days" of Genesis are not six literal 24-hour days.

- *Intelligent design*—The universe and everything in it owe their existence to a purposeful, intelligent Creator.

Science

- *Evolution*—This is an unplanned and undirected process that combines elements of random genetic changes or mutations accumulated through natural selection. *Microevolution* refers to minor variations that occur at or below the species level. *Macroevolution* refers to major innovations such as new organs, structures, or body plans above the species level.

- *Darwinism/naturalism*—With this belief, undirected mechanistic processes can account for both microevolution and macroevolution. Evolution is an unsupervised, impersonal, unpredictable, and natural process. There is no such thing as the supernatural. The universe is composed of matter in mindless motion.

A Better Way of Thinking

The reason this third option is a better way of thinking is that you take the truth of the Bible and combine it with scientific truth. When you do that, you will find nothing contradictory. As we saw in chapter 2, the order and description of Creation days is completely compatible with the facts of science concerning the appearance of the universe, the development of its structure, the appearance of life, and the development of life-forms.

And you can take this to the bank. The more true science learns about the *theories* of Darwinism and macroevolution, the more science has reason to doubt their validity. By contrast, the more science learns about the facts of our universe, the more those facts line up in perfect harmony with the biblical record.

A Brief History of Primates, Hominids, and Humans

Now let's turn our attention to the subject of this chapter: human life. How did we all begin? First we're going to look at the *facts* of science, and then compare them to what Darwinism says and what the Bible says. Let's begin with those creatures commonly believed to be our ancestors.

Primates

Scientifically speaking, you are classified as a mammal (the age of mammals began about 65 million years ago following the extinction of the dinosaurs). Within the class *Mammalia* is the order called *Primates,* a group of over 230 species of mammals that includes lemurs, tarsiers, monkeys, apes, and humans. That's right. You are a primate. But hear us out. Just because you are classified as a primate doesn't mean you descended from primates. The facts of science do not support that. Darwinism may tell you that, but science doesn't. Don't be fooled into believing that Darwinism equals science.

A Common Designer, Not a Common Ancestry

Some scientists are quick to point out that the DNA of humans and apes is remarkably similar. In fact, we share 98.5 percent of our genetic makeup with primates. But as Charles Colson points out in *How Now Shall We Live?* "What an amazing difference that 1.5 percent seems to make." Even the most "intelligent" monkeys can perform rudimentary tasks at best (not much different from a dog or a dolphin). Otherwise, they pretty much act like the animals they are, responding to basic biological urges (eating, sleeping, swinging, picking bugs off each other). Humans, on the other hand, possess a vastly superior intelligence, unique among primates. If humans evolved from monkeys, you would think that somewhere along the way you would find a primate possessing intelligence somewhere between a chimpanzee and Albert Einstein (sorry, Howard Stern doesn't qualify).

> The similarity between primates and humans—whether it's our DNA or physical appearance—does not necessarily prove a common ancestry. A more likely explanation is this: The similarity shows a common designer.

The Search for the Missing Link

Scientifically speaking, the only way to prove that humans are descended from apes is to find fossils that show a transition—a link—between monkeys, apes, and humans. Ever since Darwinism became the accepted scientific *theory* (not fact) for how humans got here, scientists have been searching for this missing link. Despite what you were taught in school—despite what Darwinists will try to tell you now—paleoanthropologists (those who study human ancestors) have not uncovered the transitional fossils linking monkeys to apes to humans. (For that matter, science has never found transitional fossil evidence for a link between any major forms.)

When Darwinists Get Desperate

For more than 40 years, Darwinists believed they had found the missing link. In 1912 an amateur geologist by the name of Charles Dawson discovered fossil evidence of a creature with the jaw of an ape and the skull of a human. Dawson called his creature *Piltdown man* and promptly brought it to the British museum, where scientists announced to the world that the elusive transitional link between apes and man had been found.

What the world didn't know was that Piltdown man was a hoax. Someone had cleverly taken the jaw of an ape and the skull of a man and combined the two. The sad part of this story is that the Piltdown fossil fooled the experts in spite of indications that it was a fake, since it fit Darwin's theory. This so-called "evidence" that man had descended from apes was taught in schools around the world for 40 years until the fraud was universally exposed and acknowledged.

Scientists have found primate-like fossils that date back 60 million years. The fossil record shows that primitive monkeys and apes appeared 25 million years ago. The first ape to move from the trees to the plain was *Ramapithecus*. Fossil fragments indicate that this apelike creature lived around 12 million years ago. In the early 1950s, paleoanthropologists believed that *Ramapithecus* was the missing link leading to man, but the evidence just wasn't conclusive. Now scientists believe *Ramapithecus* was the ancestor of modern orangutans.

In fact, there are no primate-like ape fossils to be found anywhere after eight million years ago. Modern apes—including gorillas, orangutans, and chimpanzees—seem to come out of nowhere.

Hominids

Anthropologists define *hominid* as a member of the family of humans. Technically, hominids walk on two feet (that makes them *bipedal*) and are characterized by an erect posture. All humans are hominids, but all hominids aren't human.

Australopithecus (southern ape) is the name scientists gave to the first hominids, which lived about five million years ago. There were three species of *Australopiths* (abbreviated by the letter *A*)—

- *A. afarensis*
- *A. africanus*
- *A. robustus*

In the 1960s and 1970s, paleoanthropologists were confident that one or two of these hominids were the ancestors of *Homo sapiens* (that's us). The most famous *A. afarensis* was "Lucy," discovered in 1974 by leading paleoanthropologist Donald Johanson. This little hominid was the leading candidate for the missing link, until further study questioned the evidence connecting Lucy with other species. Johanson admitted in 1981 that "science has not known, and does not know today, just how or when the all-important transition from ape to hominid took place."

Paleontology does not demonstrate a slow, gradual, rectilinear ascent of organic entities from the lower to the higher but shows that all kinds of species existed side by side from the beginning.

—Herman Bavinck

A scientific hypothesis worthy of consideration is that either *A. afarensis* or *A. africanus* is the fossil ancestor of the chimpanzee, and *A. robustus* is the fossil ancestor of the gorilla. In other words, these celebrated hominids are simply the missing extinct ancestors of modern-day apes. As for *Homo habilis* and *Homo erectus,* two hominids that scientists usually put in the human family tree, they may likely have had no direct connection to humans.

Creation, Extinction, Creation

Many Christians assume that once God created something, it was here to stay. They incorrectly believe that extinction has occurred only as a result of man's irresponsible behavior and the weight of sin on the world. That is partly true, but the fact is that extinctions took place before humans arrived on the scene.

Dr. Hugh Ross writes: "Throughout six creation epochs or creation days, God created new species and replaced species that went extinct through the normal operation of physical laws (thermodynamics, gravity, electromagnetism, and so forth) and through environmental changes preparatory to humans' arrival and survival."

Creatures of various kinds—including primates and hominids—went extinct through the natural physical laws that God created to govern the universe. But He replaced them with new species that "matched or outstripped the extinction rate." Then came humans, God's final act of creation, followed by the seventh day of Creation. From this point forward God "rested" from His creation activity, and the introduction of new species stopped. Once again the Bible is consistent with science, which shows "a roughly zero rate" of speciation.

What About the Cavemen?

Ah yes, the cavemen. Did these brutish creatures with clubs, animal skins, and sloping foreheads exist, or are they as phony as

Fred Flintstone? Well, neither science nor the Bible calls them "cavemen," but the evidence for hominid cave dwellers certainly exists, and nothing about their existence contradicts the Bible.

*N*eanderthals and Cro-Magnons lived between 200,000 and 30,000 years ago. They hunted, used tools and fire, and gathered in groups. Neanderthals were heavily muscled, especially in the neck and shoulders, with massive brow ridges over their eyes. Their noses, jaws, and teeth protruded far forward, but their lower jaw sloped back without a chin. Not the sort you would want to meet in a back alley on a dark night. Neanderthals went extinct 30,000 years ago and are not thought to be ancestors of modern humans.

Cro-Magnons appeared in Eurasia 100,000 years ago. (They possibly originated in Africa or the Near East. Some of the earliest fossils are found in caves on Mount Carmel and near Nazareth.) They made advanced stone tools, were very accomplished hunters, and possessed language and buried their dead. Cro-Magnons are best known for their incredible artistic ability, painting beautiful three-dimensional drawings of animals on cave walls in France and Spain. They were fully modern in appearance, and anthropologists accordingly classify them as *Homo sapiens sapiens* (the same as us).

According to Hugh Ross, the "cavemen" probably lacked the five characteristics of a "spiritual component" which are unique to all humans who have ever lived:

1. Awareness of a moral code "written" or impressed within a conscience

2. Concerns about life and life after death

3. Desire to communicate with and worship a higher being

4. Consciousness of self

5. Capacity to recognize truth and absolutes

Paleoanthropologist Richard Leakey recognized these unique human characteristics. He wrote: "Our sense of justice, our need for aesthetic pleasure, our imaginative flights, and our penetrating self-awareness all combine to create an indefinable spirit which I believe is the 'soul.' " Darwinists have never been able to explain why human beings alone have this "soul."

Do you see the distinction here? Darwinist evolutionist theory claims—and cannot prove—that one species evolved into another, branching out like a tree:

Darwinian Predictions Chart

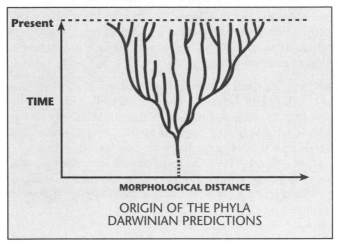

ORIGIN OF THE PHYLA
DARWINIAN PREDICTIONS

Scientific *fact* (based on fossil evidence) shows that new forms of life appeared suddenly, just like the Bible says:

The Fossil Evidence Chart

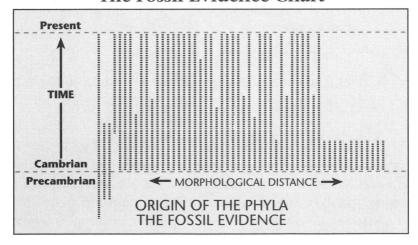

ORIGIN OF THE PHYLA
THE FOSSIL EVIDENCE

All of the evidence points to a directed, planned process created by an intelligent designer. The notion that the universe and everything in it came about and developed on its own through a random, mechanistic, undirected process doesn't *just* contradict the Bible. It contradicts the major patterns in the fossil record.

God's Crowning Achievement

After creating every kind of animal on Day 6, God wasn't finished. Picture it: The universe is filled with galaxies, stars, and planets, all perfectly positioned for optimum life on planet Earth, which is now wonderfully adorned with atmosphere, water, and land. Organic chemicals are in perfect balance, oxygen is plentiful, vegetation is abundant, and the earth is full of living creatures. The stage is set for God's final act of creation: humankind.

---

*W*hen and Where
Did the First Humans Appear?

Dr. Hugh Ross reports that some of the characteristics that identify human beings, such as religious relics and altars, date back only as far as 24,000 years "at most." Art containing "indisputable spiritual content" dates back only 5000 years. Therefore, he estimates that humans created by God and in His image appeared somewhere between 5000 and 24,000 years ago, which is completely consistent with the dates of science, young earth creationists, and old earth creationists.

Furthermore, John Wiester writes that "the first animal husbandry, the first agriculture, and first towns, and the beginnings of civilization occurred in ancient Israel and Mesopotamia." Not coincidentally, this is the same geographic area described by the Bible as the center of human origin.

The creation of human beings marks a whole new chapter and a whole new way of creating for God. Hebrew scholar John Sailhamer lists a series of "subtle contrasts" between the way God created humans and the way He created everything else on this planet.

Creation of Humankind	Creation of Everything Else
God's command is personal: *"Let us make people"* (Genesis 1:26).	God's commands are impersonal: *"Let there be light"* (Genesis 1:3).
Humans are made in God's image (Genesis 1:26).	Creatures are made according to their "own kind" (Genesis 1:25).
God specifies gender: "Male and female he created them" (Genesis 1:27).	God doesn't specify gender.
Humans are given the responsibility to be "masters over all life" (Genesis 1:26).	No creature has mastery over any part of God's creation.

There are two aspects to our uniqueness as humans. First, we are different from the rest of God's creation. Second, we are like our Creator. We are the only beings in the universe created in the image and likeness of God.

The Uniqueness of Being Human

Three thousand years ago King David wrote in the Psalms:

> *When I look at the night sky and see the work of your fingers—the moon and the stars you have set in place—what are mortals that you should think of us, mere humans that you should care for us?* (Psalm 8:3-4).

We could use a little more of this kind of wonder and humility in our modern world. Human beings have become so impressed with themselves and their accomplishments that God has been pushed out of the picture. To many people, if God exists at all, it's to serve us and to help us become even greater. How arrogant we are as a species! The truth is that the same God who created the incredible universe also created us. Not only that, but He created us with His divine imprint. Like David, we should be humble and grateful before God, not proud and independent.

Pastor Gilbert Bilezikian lists three qualities that tell us what it means to be created in God's image:

> **1. *The image of transcendence.*** Only God exists apart from and completely autonomous from the created world (that's what it means to be transcendent), but there is a sense in which humans exist apart from the rest of creation. God carefully formed us from the dust of the ground, just like He formed vegetation and living creatures (Genesis 1:11-12,24). But He did something completely different with His human creation. God personally "breathed into it the breath of life" (Genesis 2:7), which means that Adam, the first human, and all humans thereafter would be "endowed with personhood." This is so we would be both responsive to God and responsible for God's creation (Genesis 1:26-28).

> **2. *The image of a dynamic being.*** When God created humankind, He did so "within himself as a Tri-unity of persons (Genesis 1:26)." Bilezikian also writes, "Since humans were made in God's image, it was inevitable that the plurality within his being would be reflected in a plurality of human persons. God in community created humans in community." God is a "plurality of persons." He is three Persons in one: God the Father, God the Son, and God the Holy Spirit (that's the Trinity). Because humans are created in this image of plurality, they have a plurality as well: male and female. And God has given them the ability and the responsibility to "bring forth life made in the image of God."

As human beings created in God's image, reproduction is not our only responsibility. God wants us to produce as well. Work is not a curse, but a privilege (Genesis 2:15). God created for six days, and then "on the seventh day, having finished his task, God rested from all his work"

(Genesis 2:2). If God worked for our benefit, we need to work for His benefit (and for ours). And a large part of that work involves taking care of His creation. God wants us to be stewards and users—not abusers—of His world.

3. *The image of absolute goodness.* "It is impossible for humans to duplicate perfectly the holiness of God, since they do not have his transcendence," writes Bilezikian. "However, by virtue of the goodness of God's creation, humans have a share in that goodness." At the end of His creative process, God declared everything He had made as "excellent in every way" (Genesis 1:31). Part of that excellence and goodness was our free will. God could have made us like robots who had no choice but to respond to Him and do everything He says. But God in His perfect goodness and wisdom gave us the capacity to make our own moral choices.

What the Image of God Is Not

Nobody has ever seen God, because God is a spirit. So being in God's image doesn't mean we look like Him. It means we are *like* God. It means that we have God's imprint. We are His design. Theologian Wayne Grudem says it this way: "The fact that man is in the image of God means that man is like God and represents God." The Hebrew word for *image* refers to something that is *similar* but not identical to the things it represents.

Three Limits of God's Image

Bilezikian reminds us that despite our greatness as unique creations and image-bearers of God, we humans were created with some limitations. In a nutshell, we are "finite, limited, and vulnerable," three qualities expressed in these three limits:

1. *Human dependency.* Unlike God, humans are not self-sufficient or self-existent. Our most basic needs are for food, shelter, and human companionship. God carefully and lovingly provided all of these for our benefit and enjoyment (Genesis 1:29;2:9,18).

2. *Human mortality.* God is not affected by death because He is transcendent. God is the source of life. Unlike God, humans are vulnerable to death, just like the rest of His creation. This is a little tricky, so stay with us. God did not create His image-bearers to die, but He created them with the capacity to die. It was impossible for humans to be immune to death, because only God is immune to death, and we are not God, and neither are we equal to God.

   The tree of the knowledge of good and evil (Genesis 2:17) wasn't placed in the Garden of Eden to tempt humanity (that was Satan's doing). The tree was placed in the center of the Garden as a warning to Adam, as humanity's representative, that disobedience to God will lead to death.

3. *Human corruptibility.* Humans may have been created in the image of God's absolute goodness, but human goodness is not absolute. In other words, God created us to connect with Him, but He also created us with the capacity to break that connection. Human corruptibility isn't a surprise to God. It's the way He created us. God knew about human corruptibility, and He carefully explained to Adam what would happen if he disobeyed God's warning (Genesis 2:16-17).

Bilezikian points out that human dependency, mortality, and corruptibility don't mean that God blew it. He didn't create an imperfect world. "It only means that a vast difference exists between the Creator and the image-bearers." When we recognize that difference—especially in light of the consequences that come when God's human creation disobeys God's perfect plan—then the words of David take on even greater meaning.

When you consider how we have messed up God's plan, jeopardized His creation, and generally thumbed our human noses at His unconditional love for us, you have to wonder why God even bothers with us. But He does. He continues to love us, continues to care for us, and continues to draw us to Himself. Why? It goes to the heart of why God made us in the first place.

*I*mage-Bearers Versus Naked Apes

Contrast this noble purpose for humankind as expressed in the Bible with the bleak purpose proposed by Darwinism. Sure, Darwinists will tell you that humans can find great purpose by serving each other and improving the environment (both of which are noble purposes, by the way), but don't let their optimism fool you. At its heart the biblical view of humankind is that all human life is to be valued equally because all humans are created in the image of God. The Bible also tells us that in spite of our corruptibility, each of us has an eternal destiny, which gives us dignity before our Creator and with each other.

Contrast this view with that of Darwinism and naturalism. God does not exist in the natural world. He is not our Creator, and therefore He is not a factor in our world or our lives. Charles Colson writes, "If we were not created by God—and therefore are not bound by his laws—if we are simply the most advanced of the primates, why shouldn't we do whatever we choose?" When you get right down to it, in the Darwinist system of thought, we really are nothing more than "naked apes."

Why Did God Create Us?

It's important for all of us to remember that God didn't need to create us, yet He did. Why? This is a question that has puzzled kings, philosophers, theologians, and plain old people like us for thousands of years. Because He is God, He doesn't need anything—not the universe, not the earth, not even us. God didn't create us because He was lonely. Wayne Grudem reminds us that there was "perfect love and fellowship among members of the Trinity for all eternity (John 17:5,24)." God has all the company He needs without us.

Yet He did create the heavens and the earth and everything in it—including us—with incredible precision, care, and purpose. So what was that purpose?

*A*t some future time period...the civilized races of man will almost certainly exterminate, and replace, the savage races throughout the world.

—Charles Darwin in
The Descent of Man

More than 350 years ago some very wise theologians wrote a document known as the "Shorter Catechism of the Westminster Confession." This statement is generally accepted as the most accurate description of the "chief end" or the purpose of humanity: "Man's chief and highest end is to glorify God, and to fully enjoy Him forever."

God Created Us for His Own Glory

We don't have to wonder if this is the reason God created us. He said so Himself:

> *All who claim me as their God will come, for I have made them for my glory. It was I who created them* (Isaiah 43:7).

The apostle Paul echoed this when he wrote to the church at Rome:

> *For everything comes from him; everything exists by his power and is intended for his glory. To him be glory forevermore. Amen* (Romans 11:36).

And That's What We Should Do

Knowing why God created us simplifies things, doesn't it? We don't have to wonder why we're here and what we should do. As Paul wrote to the Corinthian church:

> *Whatever you eat or drink or whatever you do, you must do all for the glory of God* (1 Corinthians 10:31).

Wayne Grudem observes that this single fact "guarantees that our lives are significant." Think about it. When you realize that God didn't need to create you and doesn't need you for anything, you might conclude that you really aren't much more than a naked ape. But when you read the Bible and discover that you were created to glorify God, it shows that you are singularly important to the actual Creator of the universe.

God doesn't ask you to glorify Him for His benefit. He created you this way for *your* benefit, indicating that you are important to *God Himself*. "This is the final definition of genuine importance or significance to our lives," writes Grudem. "If we are truly important to God for all eternity, then what greater measure of importance or significance could we want?"

"What's That Again?"

1. Many people believe they are stuck with only two options when it comes to the origins of the universe and human life:

   Option #1: Believe what the Bible says—even though it doesn't provide scientific explanations—because you believe in God.

   Option #2: Believe in science—even though it leaves God out of the picture—because it presents the facts about human origins.

2. There is a third and better option. You can believe the Bible because it's true, and you can believe science as long as it's true.

3. The similarities between primates and humans indicate a common designer rather than a common ancestry.

4. Scientists have yet to discover a single piece of credible fossil evidence showing the transition from apes to humans.

5. The unique creation of humankind in the image of God was God's crowning creative achievement.

6. These three qualities tell us what it means to be created in God's image:

   • The image of transcendence

   • The image of a dynamic being

   • The image of absolute goodness

7. God created humans with three major limitations:

   • Human dependency

   • Human mortality

   • Human corruptibility

8. The chief end of humanity is to glorify God and to enjoy Him forever.

Dig Deeper

We found a book written more than 15 years ago by a French theologian to be very helpful for this chapter (no, we didn't read it in French). *In the Beginning* by Henri Blocher has some great insights into the events of Creation, especially the creation of humankind.

By the time we're done with this book, we will have used every book written by Dr. Hugh Ross. *The Genesis Question* was particularly helpful for our study of the order of the Creation days, the question of creation and extinction, and the creation of human beings.

Christianity 101 is a basic book for your library. Gilbert Bilezikian is a teaching pastor at Willow Creek Community Church in Chicago, and he has a wonderful way of explaining theology clearly (our kind of guy). We leaned heavily on his chapter "The Doctrine of Human Beings" for this chapter.

If you were going to have only one volume of systematic theology (these are very thick books written by very smart people), then we would suggest Wayne Grudem's *Systematic Theology* (these academic guys always give their books such creative titles). He is clear, fairly easy to follow, and practical. His chapters on the creation and nature of man are great.

■ ■ ■

*Q*uestions for *R*eflection and *D*iscussion

1. As you have progressed through your education (both formal and informal), have you had to separate your belief in the Bible from what you believe in science? Explain. How has this hindered your spiritual growth? How has this hindered your interest in science?

2. Why have some Christians been so reluctant to take the truth of the Bible and combine it with scientific truth? Why have some scientists been so reluctant to do the same?

3. We have shown where Darwinists have become desperate in the defense of their beliefs. Have Christians ever become desperate in the defense of their beliefs? Why are such tactics unnecessary?

4. Some Creationists take exception with the idea that extinction and death took place before God created humanity. Do you think death took place before humanity sinned? Explain your answer.

5. How are we like our Creator? How are we different? Does knowing that we are like our Creator give us certain privileges? Does it give us certain responsibilities? What are they?

6. Think like a Darwinist for a moment. What is the chief end of humankind? What is our noble purpose?

7. Someone once said, "When we glorify God, we make Him look good." What are some of the ways you can make God look good?

■ ■ ■

Moving On...

This chapter on the creation of humankind is the perfect springboard for the next chapter on the significance and meaning of the human race. It's one thing to know that our purpose is to glorify God, and quite another to find our meaning in God. In the next chapter we'll dig into the realm of the human mind. What have people thought about God and the supernatural realm? Where do ideas about God come from? And in the end, does it really matter what we think about God, as long as we're sincere?

So put on your thinking cap and prepare to think big as you consider what it means to have meaning.

Chapter 9

> It is incomprehensible that God should exist, and it is incomprehensible that He should not exist.
>
> —*Blaise Pascal*

One of the wonders of God's creative process is the human brain. Not only did God create human beings in His image, but He endowed each person with the ability to think and be self-aware.

Your brain also gives you the ability to be aware of God. In fact, your brain has been programmed with a special "deity chip," so you have no choice but to think about God. The question is: What do you think about God? Is He just a concept, or is He a presence in your life? It doesn't matter that you can't see Him. Your brain can't see either. What it does is think and process and take care of the things that keep you alive.

Your brain makes you who you are and gives you the capacity to know who God is. There can be no higher purpose than that!

The Human Mind:
What Do You
Think About God?

*A*t one time or another, even the most committed believer in God has doubts—even if they are very small ones—about whether God really exists. You may not regularly stay awake at night worrying that God isn't there, but you have to admit that at least once in your life this thought has crossed your mind: *What if this whole thing is an illusion? What if Darwin was right? What if we really did come from the prebiotic soup?*

If this has happened to you, don't worry. You're not in danger of losing your grip on reality (or your salvation, for that matter). What you're going through is a very natural process. It's called doubting, and it's part of being human—whether you believe in God or not.

Doubt and Faith

The great contemporary writer Philip Yancey, in his very good book *Reaching for the Invisible God*, explains why we doubt and why it's okay. "Doubt always co-exists with faith, for in the presence of certainty who would need faith at all?"

We're going to talk about faith in the next chapter. In this chapter we're going to talk about doubt and why it's important to our discussion about the universe and how it began and how you can find meaning in it all. (Hint: If you follow through on your doubts, they will inevitably lead you to God, no matter how far away from Him you feel.)

You Are Going to Wonder

There may be times in your life when you are absolutely sure of God's existence and His present power in the universe and in your life. But there may also be times when you wonder if God is even real. Usually this happens during a time of personal crisis. You say to yourself, "If God is out there, why doesn't He help me?" Or you might read about some kind of horrible war or natural calamity, and in your helplessness cry out, "If God is a real presence in the world, why do so many bad things happen?"

---

*W*ithout somehow destroying me in the process, how could God reveal himself in a way that would leave no room for doubt? If there were no room for doubt, there would be no room for me.

—Frederick Buechner

Is it simply the circumstances of our lives and the state of the world that cause us to doubt God, or is there more to it than that? Although circumstances are certainly a factor, your view of God is probably much more important. If you see God as a celestial Santa Claus who gives you good things when you've been nice and withholds them when you've been naughty, then your doubts come from your emotions. On the other hand, if God is an impersonal idea to you who exists only because you think about Him, then your doubts are more intellectual in nature.

It doesn't matter whether you embrace God wholeheartedly, or whether you are still skeptical about this whole business of God creating the universe. You are going to have doubts. You are going to wonder, *Is this really true?*

Still Only Two Choices

The choice of what to believe isn't complicated. There are still only two choices. Either God exists and He created the universe, or He doesn't exist and He didn't create the universe. But the process of how you get to either choice can be difficult. Just because you have already made a choice doesn't mean you're not thinking about whether or not you made the *right* choice. It's very natural to want confirmation. We want to be certain that we've made the right choice about God and everything that goes with it.

Blaise Pascal, the very brilliant philosopher and mathematician, said, "It is incomprehensible that God should exist, and it is incomprehensible that He should not exist." Now there's a guy caught in the middle! When he considered the evidence about God's existence, Pascal concluded that there was "too much to deny, too little to be sure."

You Think, Therefore You Are

You may have heard someone say, "It's impossible to absolutely know whether God exists, so why bother?" This notion has its roots in the thinking of Immanuel Kant, an eighteenth-century philosopher who decided that the existence of God is a question beyond our ability to answer because it can't be proven without doubt.

As powerful a thinker as Kant was, he wasn't the only brilliant European philosopher who seriously pondered the existence of God. René Descartes, another French philosopher and mathematician, decided that the whole world was full of doubt, but he came away with a different and very significant conclusion. Descartes said that his doubting meant that he was thinking, and the fact that he was thinking meant that he existed, leading him to make his famous statement: "I think, therefore I am."

This may seem like a silly intellectual exercise, but it's very important to our discussion. Here's how R. C. Sproul puts it: "To be able to say with certainty that *something* exists is crucial. There are numerous reasons why a thing might exist, but...the existence of something gives us a rational basis for assuming the existence of God."

A Mind Is a Terrible Thing to Waste

See, there's a reason why it's important to think (and all this time you thought it was a waste of time). Thinking proves that you exist! (A reverse corollary statement: If nobody knows you exist, try thinking more.) And your thinking is the only way you will understand that God exists as well.

John Polkinghorne is one of the world's leading thinkers in the area of science and religion (he was a professor of mathematical physics at Cambridge University before resigning his chair to study theology). In his book *Belief in God in an Age of Science*, Polkinghorne agrees that you can't absolutely prove the existence of God. But he also says—

> There are two locations where general hints of the divine presence might be expected to be seen most clearly. One is the vast cosmos itself, with its fifteen-billion-year history of evolving development following the big bang. The other is the "thinking reed" of humanity, so insignificant in physical scale but, as Pascal said, superior to all the stars because it alone knows them and itself.

Our surplus intellectual capacity, enabling us to comprehend the microworld of quarks and gluons and the macroworld of big bang cosmology, is on such a scale that it beggars belief that this is simply a fortunate by-product of the struggle for life.

—John Polkinghorne

The very idea that you exist and can think about God and the universe means that you *should*. Your brain is there for a reason, and we're going to take a wild guess and say it's not for picking numbers on a lottery ticket. The highest form of thinking is to think about God and the universe. Who is God, what has He done, and how can you relate to Him? A mind really is a terrible thing to waste, especially if you're not using it to think about God.

Evidence for God

What we want to do is get your mind in gear by reviewing the two main pieces of evidence for the existence of God from the universe. Then we want to present two additional pieces of evidence for the existence of God that arise from you as a thinking person. As powerful as these proofs are, they are only one part of what it takes to truly believe in God. The other part is faith (which we're going to deal with in chapter 10).

If we were writing an equation for belief in God, it would look like this:

Evidence + Faith = Belief

Now let's look at the evidence.

The Evidence from the Universe

These first two pieces of evidence will be a review of previous chapters.

> 1. *The evidence of cause and effect.* Often called the *cosmological* argument (from the Greek word *kosmos*, meaning "order, world, universe"), this piece of logic from chapter 1 states that you can't get something from nothing (remember *ex nihilo, nihil fit?*). This is an incontrovertible piece of evidence that applies to science as well as religion (we just *had* to use the word *incontrovertible* one more time in this book). The universe is an effect that exists, and because it is an effect, there must be a cause. Effects don't happen by themselves.
>
> As you go back further and further in the "chain of causes," you must come to a First Big Cause that got the whole thing going, and that First Big Cause must itself be uncaused. The only possible candidate for the First Big

Cause is God, who is Himself uncaused, or self-existent. Chance didn't cause the universe, the universe didn't cause itself, and God didn't cause Himself. All of those are rational impossibilities.

A parallel argument to the evidence of cause and effect is the evidence of the beginning. The universe had a beginning at a single point in time. Scientists haven't always known this, but they know it now, and they can prove it. If the universe had a beginning, something outside the universe must have "caused" it into existence. The only candidate for this "something" is God, the great Beginner.

> *God, the LORD, created the heavens and stretched them out. He created the earth and everything in it. He gives breath and life to everyone in all the world"* (Isaiah 42:5).

2. *The evidence of design and purpose.* Sometimes called the *teleological* argument (from the Greek word *telos*, meaning "end" or "goal"), this piece of evidence says that the obvious order and design in the universe—from the fine tuning in space to the fine tuning in your body—point to an intelligent designer.

Two hundred years ago, theologian William Paley stated his famous "watchmaker" theory, which basically says that a watch without a watchmaker is less incredible than a creation without a Creator.

---

*I*t is impossible to account for the creation of the universe without the agency of a Supreme Being.

—George Washington

We can see the evidence of design in many aspects of science—criminology, anthropology, archaeology, and astronomy. There's no reason why we can't apply the evidence of design to theology as well. Imagine if we discovered a Ramada Inn on Mars. We wouldn't automatically assume that it just evolved over time. We would correctly conclude that some intelligent designer (in this case an enterprising hotel chain) put it there (and then, of course, the government would figure out a way to impose property taxes).

A parallel argument to the evidence of design and order is the concept of irreducible complexity, which points out that certain things in the universe (the human eye, for example) are so complex that every part has to be present and functioning at the same time in order for those things to work.

From the time the world was created, people have seen the earth and sky and all that God made. They can clearly see his invisible qualities—his eternal power and divine nature. So they have no excuse whatsoever for not knowing God (Romans 1:20).

The Problem with Physical Evidence

There are at least two dangers in relying solely on the physical evidence to prove the existence of God. First, thinking people will draw different conclusions from the evidence. For example, even though the vast majority of scientists now believe the evidence points to a beginning for the universe, physicist Andrei Linde of Stanford University believes the universe is eternal and "self-reproducing" through a series of big bangs. And the renowned neo-Darwinist Richard Dawkins disagrees that the complexity of living organisms proves that a Creator exists. Using the watchmaker analogy, he writes, "All appearances to the contrary, the only watchmaker in nature is the blind forces of physics, albeit deployed in a very special way....It is the *blind* watchmaker."

To suppose that the eye, with so many parts all working together... could have been formed by natural selection, seems, I freely confess, absurd in the highest degree.

—Charles Darwin

We don't think these guys are right, of course, but they would say the same thing about us. The point is that physical evidence isn't always 100 percent conclusive, especially when it comes to God. If it were, then 100 percent of all people would believe.

> *A* God who would let us prove his existence would be an idol.
>
> —Dietrich Bonhoeffer

The second danger with relying solely on the physical evidence to prove God's existence is that you can't put God under a microscope. You can't view Him through a telescope, either. As Philip Yancey writes, "God is infinite, intangible, and invisible."

- *The Infinite God.* Let's be very clear about this. The universe is a big place. Very big. Incomprehensibly big. But God is even bigger. In fact, when it comes to size and scope, there's no comparison. We have an idea as to how big the universe is, but with God we have no idea, because you can't measure God. This is because while the universe is finite, God is *infinite*. Compared to God, the universe is the size of an atom, and even that isn't completely accurate. There are degrees of size, but infinity has no degree.

- *The Intangible God.* The literal meaning of *intangible* is "not easily grasped by the mind." That's God! We can talk all we want about thinking about God, but in the end we can't completely get our minds around Him. God has given us the ability to *know* Him, but try as we may, we can never fully *comprehend* Him.

  "My thoughts are completely different from yours," says the LORD. "And my ways are far beyond anything you could imagine. For just as the heavens are higher than the earth, so are my ways higher than your ways and my thoughts higher than your thoughts" (Isaiah 55:8).

- ***The Invisible God.*** No one has seen God because God is Spirit (John 4:24). This is not to say that God hasn't revealed Himself. He has been very generous about letting us "see" Him:

  - Through nature (Romans 1:20)

  - Through the prophets (Hebrews 1:1)

  - Through His written word (2 Timothy 3:16)

  - Through Jesus Christ, His Son (Hebrews 1:2)

But God is invisible. He can't be seen and He can't be measured. That's what makes Him God. We should have the same attitude as the apostle Paul, who wrote:

> *Glory and honor to God forever and ever. He is the eternal*
> *King, the unseen one who never dies; He alone is God.*
> *Amen* (1 Timothy 1:17).

We need to get away from the human tendency to put God in a box, where we've got Him all figured out. The advancements of science have been a great help in giving us evidence for our faith, but scientific evidence can also make us arrogant. Consider this quote from Dr. Evan Harris Walker, a theoretical physicist: "It now appears that research underway offers the possibility of establishing the existence of an agency having the properties and characteristics ascribed to the religious concept of God."

God is a circle whose center is everywhere and circumference is nowhere.

—Timaeus of Locris

How mighty and intelligent we are! We have proved God's existence. Yippee! Give the human race a medal for intelligence and good sense. Hogwash! God doesn't need a science lab to prove He exists, any more than you need a birth certificate to prove you exist. He exists because He is God, and above Him there is no other.

Here's a quote we like much better from good old John Polkinghorne: "We are not now looking to the physical world for hints of God's existence but to God's existence as an aid for understanding why things have developed in the physical world in the manner that they have."

The Evidence from You

Naturally, we aren't suggesting that you throw out the physical evidence. God has allowed you to see Him in the universe He created. But He has also given you reason to believe He exists from the person He created (that would be you).

1. *The evidence of morality.* We live in a time when right and wrong get a little fuzzy at times. What's right for one person, we are told, may be wrong for someone else, and vice versa. This is called moral relativism. J. P. Moreland, a professor of philosophy at Talbot Theological Seminary, defines it this way: "Moral relativism implies that moral propositions are not simply true or false. Rather, the truth values (true or false) of moral principles themselves are relative to the beliefs of a given culture."

The problem with moral relativism is that when push comes to shove, every single person will argue for what he or she thinks is right. This evidence for morality isn't there by chance. This sense of right and wrong, which C.S. Lewis called "a clue to the meaning of the universe," is in you and everyone else because God put it there. He built us to know right from wrong, even if we don't always choose what's right.

> *They show that in their hearts they know right from wrong. They demonstrate that God's law is written within them, for their own consciences either accuse them or tell them they are doing what is right* (Romans 2:14-15).

2. *The evidence of thinking about God.* Here's something to consider: If God doesn't exist, why do we think about Him? Not just a few of us, but all of us think about God.

"The Professor and the Stolen Stereo"

The problem with moral relativism is that even the most open-minded and "tolerant" person at some point puts his or her foot down—morally speaking. Dr. Moreland tells the story of a conversation he had with a student in his dorm room. The student insisted that no one should force his or her views on other people since everything is relative. Without saying anything to refute the student's statement, Dr. Moreland picked up the student's stereo and walked out the door. The student protested vigorously, demanding that Dr. Moreland put his stereo back where it belonged.

"Surely you aren't going to force on me your belief that it is wrong to steal your stereo," Dr. Moreland said. "You know what I think?" he continued. "I think that you espouse relativism in areas of your life where it's convenient, say in sexual morality, or in areas about which you do not care, but when it comes to someone stealing your stereo or criticizing your own moral hobbyhorses, I suspect that you become a moral absolutist pretty quickly, don't you?"

The student sheepishly agreed.

Even the atheist, in trying to deny God's existence, has to think about God. The evidence is clear from studies of human history that spiritual awareness—the God idea—has been there from the beginning. It's what sets us apart from the animals and nature. This constant awareness of God through the ages and across all cultures gives proof for His existence because only God could have put that idea in our heads.

For the truth about God is known to them instinctively. God has put this knowledge in their hearts (Romans 1:19).

Humankind has struggled tirelessly in its effort to deny God or to come up with alternative gods. But this speaks to the rebellion of God's created beings to their Creator rather than the nonexistence of God.

Instead of believing what they knew was the truth about God, they deliberately chose to believe lies. So they worshiped the things God made but not the Creator himself, who is to be praised forever (Romans 1:25).

---

*I*f no set of moral ideas were truer or better than any other, there would be no sense in preferring civilized morality to savage morality, or Christian morality to Nazi morality.

—C.S. Lewis

Who Is God?

In chapter 2 we gave you six "identities" of God as evidenced from the world God created:

1. Independent of the universe itself (transcendent)

2. All-powerful (omnipotent)

3. Timeless (eternal)

4. Supernatural (spirit)

5. Supremely intelligent (omniscient)

6. Has personality (being)

These identities tell us a lot about who God is from an objective standpoint. They can go a long way in helping us realize that God exists and that He created the universe. Hugh Ross states, "The beauty of the scientific (and other) evidences God has allowed us to discover about Him is that these meet the needs of two large segments of society." He goes on to identify these two segments:

1. Those whose barriers to faith are intellectual

2. Those whose barriers to faith come from personal pain

But what if knowing about God isn't enough? What if your doubts still linger? May we suggest that your *knowing* God hasn't turned into *experiencing* God. Francis Schaeffer, one of the great Christian thinkers of the last hundred years, put it this way: "Although rationality is important, it should never become exclusively so. Rationality is not the end of the matter."

And what is the "end of the matter"? In a word, it's *relationship*. You've got to believe that God wants a relationship with you, and you've got to believe that you need a relationship with God.

The God Who Is Near...

Yes, God is a transcendent, omnipotent, eternal, omniscient spirit Being. But God is much more. If He were just all-everything and beyond our understanding, what would that mean to us? How do you experience something you can't relate to? Now we're getting down to who God really is: *He is the God who is near.*

God isn't a far-distant entity who created the universe long ago and then let it run (or run down) on its own. And He isn't some capricious being who pops in and out of human history whenever He feels like it. He is as near as anything or anyone you could possibly know. God is near to those with intellectual barriers:

> *But you are near, O LORD, and all your commands are true* (Psalm 119:151).

And God is near to those with barriers of personal pain:

> *The LORD is close to the brokenhearted; he rescues those who are crushed in spirit* (Psalm 34:18).

> *Seek the Lord while you can find him. Call on him now while he is near* (Isaiah 55:6).

God is near, but even that's not the end of the matter. God wants you to draw near to Him. The Creator of the universe wants a relationship with you, but you have to want a relationship with Him.

A Word to the Thinking Christian

It isn't enough to come to God with just your mind. But neither should you let your mind go to waste, especially after you've made the decision to follow Christ fully. Professor Moreland lists three crucial passages of Scripture that will help you grow as a Christian:

> **Romans 12:1-2**—Don't conform to the thinking patterns of the culture. Instead, let God "transform you into a new person by changing the way you think."
>
> **Matthew 22:37-39**—The religious legalists asked Jesus to name the most important commandment. He replied, "You must love the Lord your God with all your heart, all your soul, and all your mind."
>
> **1 Peter 3:15**—You are going to get questions about your belief in God. Don't be intimidated or offended. Consider questions as an opportunity to share your faith. But you should be ready to explain what you believe and why you believe it. And that takes using your mind.

Still Not the End of the Matter

Is it enough to seek the Lord? Is it enough to draw near to God? There's still one more part of the whole experience of really knowing God. It's called *faith*.

> *So, you see, it is impossible to please God without faith. Anyone who wants to come to him must believe that there is a God and that he rewards those who sincerely seek him* (Hebrews 11:6).

And that's what the next chapter is all about.

Paul and the Philosophers

The apostle Paul was a man of towering intellect. He had the equivalent of two doctoral degrees (in religion and philosophy), so he didn't mind mixing with the intellectuals of his day. The Book of Acts records a time when Paul was walking through the city of Athens, Greece—one of the great cities of knowledge and learning of its time (in fact, the Athenians loved a vigorous argument, and they were always on the lookout for new ideas). Paul noticed an altar in the middle of the city with the inscription "To an Unknown God" (Acts 17:23). Standing in the middle of Mars Hill, where the philosophers routinely debated, Paul told a crowd of people that this "Unknown God" they were worshiping wasn't unknown at all.

> *He is the God who made the world and everything in it....He himself gives life and breath to everything, and he satisfies every need there is. From one man he created all the nations throughout the whole earth* (Acts 17:24-26).

But God is more than the Creator. He is the God who is near.

> *His purpose in all of this was that the nations should seek after God and perhaps feel their way toward him and find him—for he is not far from any one of us* (Acts 17:27).

"What's That Again?"

1. Everyone has doubts about God. Without doubt, you wouldn't need faith.

2. The fact that you have doubts means that you think, and the fact that you think means you exist. Your existence gives a rational basis for the existence of God.

3. You need evidence to believe in God, and God has given us two key pieces of evidence from the universe:

   • The evidence of cause and effect

   • The evidence of design and purpose

4. Physical evidence is not 100 percent conclusive, because God's existence can't be proven in a science experiment. He is infinite, intangible, and invisible.

5. Besides the evidence for God in the universe, there is evidence from you:

   • You know right from wrong

   • You think about God

6. God is a transcendent, omnipotent, eternal, omniscient spirit Being, but He is much more. He is the God who is near.

7. You need to seek God while He is near, by exercising faith.

Dig Deeper

If you have never read a book by Philip Yancey, we have a great suggestion. Read *Reaching for the Invisible God*. Not only will you gain a greater appreciation for this chapter, but you will also gain a greater appreciation of God.

We quoted John Polkinghorne a couple of times for good reason. He is very quotable. No one has better shown how science and belief in God are compatible. Polkinghorne's *Belief in God in an Age of Science* is a very understandable and important book.

Love Your God with All Your Mind by J. P. Moreland is one of the more intellectually challenging books on our list, but what else would you expect from a professor of philosophy whose favorite pastime is arguing with skeptics? Even though this book will challenge you mentally, it will speak directly to you spiritually.

Francis Schaeffer wrote *The God Who Is There* more than 30 years ago, and people are still discovering the power of its message. If you really want to clear the cobwebs out of your mind, get this book and read through it *slowly*. You will learn how historic Christianity can stand on its own against competing world philosophies.

Questions for Reflection and Discussion

1. Have you ever had doubts about God's existence? What were they and what did you do? Have you ever had doubts about God's ability to deal with your problems and needs? How about the problems and needs of the world? How are you dealing with these doubts?

2. What does this statement mean to you? "If there's no room for doubt, there would be no room for me."

3. Why is thinking about God the highest form of thought? What happens when people spend their lives thinking about

everything *but* God? Is it possible for a Christian to avoid thinking about God? Why or why not?

4. Which category of evidence for God is most compelling for you: The evidence from the universe or the evidence from you? Which category is more compelling to a skeptic?

5. There are at least four external ways God has let us "see" Him—through nature, the prophets, the Bible, and Jesus. What if you were to take away any one of these "windows" to God? Would there be enough evidence to believe that God exists?

6. Why is it impossible for any person to live without moral absolutes? How does the presence of human morality keep the fabric of society from unraveling?

7. Review the three Scripture passages recommended by Dr. Moreland to help you grow as a Christian: Romans 12:1-2; Matthew 22:37-39; 1 Peter 3:15. Write out the central command of each passage. How can you incorporate these three commands of Scripture into your everyday life?

▢   ▢   ▢

Moving On...

If you don't already know that the next chapter is about faith, then you didn't read this chapter. But before you turn the page, we want to assure you that our discussion about faith isn't just for the believer. There's room in chapter 10 for the skeptic as well. In fact, faith is the antidote to skepticism and doubt. And it's not just a one-time event. Faith is something you live with and depend on every day.

Chapter 10

Faith is like a toothbrush. Every man should have one and use it regularly, but he shouldn't try to use someone else's.

—*J. G. Stipe*

This chapter is all about faith (but you already knew that if you were awake while you were reading chapter 9). But don't think that we are going to get religious on you just because we are talking about faith. Actually, we don't really like religion. That might seem like a surprising statement coming from two guys who have written more than 45 books about God. But it's true. And we're pretty sure that you don't like religion either.

We think there is a distinction—a big distinction—between religion and faith. When we think of religion, we think of organizations and rules and outdated traditions. We don't think that most people are interested in finding a religion. But faith, on the other hand, has to do with where you are going to put your trust: what (or who) you are going to believe in. We think people are interested in finding a place (or person) for their faith (without the trappings of rules or regulations). Many people have decided to put their faith in God. Other people have decided to put their faith in philosophies that reject the notion of God. (That's right—even anti-God philosophies require faith.)

So whether you believe in God or are skeptical of His existence, here is our promise for this chapter: There will be no mention of religion, but there will be lots of discussion about faith. And the big question for you is, Where have you placed your faith?

Faith: Not Just a Religious Thing

You ought to be quite the science expert by now. In the last five chapters, you have gone from contemplating the magnitude of the big bang to analyzing the irreducible complexity of the human cell. You have gazed at the alignment of the planets and sipped some prebiotic soup. You've gotten down and dirty with the fossils and looked through the microscope at your own DNA.

So has all of this affected your thinking about the origins of the world and of life itself? Where do you stand on the issues of Creation and evolution? What are your opinions about the theories of Darwinism and intelligent design? Where do you come out on the "God versus no God" issue?

We don't want to be presumptuous and assume that you have become an ardent proponent of intelligent design theory. (We wouldn't want to put words in your mouth, or anything else for that matter. We learned our lesson when you gagged on the prebiotic soup.) But it seems reasonable to conclude that you might at least acknowledge that the arguments in favor of intelligent design make it a credible theory that should be discussed along with the theory of Darwinism. Too bad the mainstream Darwinists won't let you do that.

Are Faith and Intellect Mutually Exclusive?

Here's the hang-up according to the Darwinists. They say that:

- The theory of intelligent design implies the existence of an intelligent designer. (Hey! They got it right!)

- The phrase "intelligent designer" is just another name for God. (Hey! They are 2 for 2.)

- Belief in God requires faith. (These guys are really on a roll.)

- Faith is all about religion; religion is anti-intellectual and has no role in science. (Ooooh. Too bad. They blew it right at the end.)

Lest you think that we are being unreasonably harsh and unfair to the Darwinists, here are some typical quotes that reveal how they intellectually belittle anyone who concludes from the scientific evidence that God is responsible for the origin of the world and life:

> Christian theism must be rejected by any person with even a shred of respect for reason.
>
> —George H. Smith, atheist

> ACLU also opposes the inculcation of religious doctrines even if they are presented as alternatives to scientific theories. "Creation science" in all guises, for example "abrupt appearance theory" or "intelligent design theory," is just such religious doctrine.
>
> —American Civil Liberties Union

Do you see what they are doing? They are saying that belief in God requires a step of faith (because we lack actual physical evidence for this infinite, invisible, and intangible God, as you might remember from chapter 9). And they equate faith with religion, so they reject the whole God notion at the outset because they say that religion has nothing to do with science. Well, hold on a minute. This raises a few issues that ought to be discussed:

- Is faith at odds with science?

- Should intelligent design theory be rejected simply because belief in God requires an element of faith?

- What about Darwinism? Isn't some faith in that theory required in the absence of adequate evidence to prove it?

- If faith is required for belief in both intelligent design theory and Darwinism, which is the greater stretch?

Now is the perfect time to think about these questions (especially since we spend the rest of the chapter talking about them).

What Is Faith?

Let's think about what faith is—and what it isn't. Oh sure, the word can bring to mind churches, stained-glass windows, and pipe-organ music. Even Webster (the dictionary guy, not the little kid from the sitcom show of the 1980s) gives the most common definition as "the unquestioning belief in God and religious tenets." But "unquestioning belief" is not the kind of faith that seems to be required for intelligent design (and it doesn't seem to be the kind of faith that God requires either).

There doesn't have to be anything superspiritual about the definition of *faith*. When used in a nonreligious context, Webster says it just means "confidence, trust or reliance on some thing or some person." If you analyze faith from this perspective, you find that it has these principles:

- *Faith requires some evidence of reliability.* Take the chair at your dining room table where you sit for dinner every night (or the chair at Taco Bell, depending upon your family dining habits). You have sat on that chair many times before. You have evidence that it has been reliable.

Since it held you the last time, you have faith that it will hold you again (even though you might be a few burritos heavier). You don't test it first with a few 50-pound bags of cement. You just sit in it. You have faith that it will hold you.

- **Faith does not involve the disengagement of your brain.** True faith is based on research, facts, and evidence. It doesn't involve blind acceptance. You wouldn't walk into a room blindfolded and just sit anywhere with the faith that a chair would mystically appear somewhere between you and the floor. That wouldn't be faith; it would just be stupidity (and perhaps require a few appointments at your neighborhood chiropractor).

Faith is not trying to believe something regardless of the evidence. Faith is daring to do something regardless of the consequences.

—Sherwood Eddy

Faith Is What You Think...and More

The Darwinists are correct when they say that belief in God requires faith. But they imply that faith requires the willful suspension of rational thought, thereby making every person who believes in the Bible an irrational, illogical lunatic (or at least a naive dunderhead). However, God doesn't want blithering idiots either. He requires a faith that involves your mind (knowledge), your spirit (trust), and your heart (will).

- **Knowledge:** We think Webster would have been more accurate if he had defined *faith* as an *unwavering* belief in God instead of an *unquestioning* belief. Asking questions is an important part of formulating faith. ("Where is the chair?" "How was it constructed?" "Has it held people of similar girth in the past without breaking?") Knowledge is a necessary component of faith. In discussing the role of faith in salvation, Bible scholar Harold Lindsell emphasized the importance of knowledge in the process: "No man can be saved without knowing something. Faith is not ignorance; it is not closing one's eyes to the facts. Faith is never afraid to look the truth squarely in the face."

- **Trust:** When the Bible talks about faith and belief, it means much more than mere confidence in knowledge of a fact. ("I am really, really sure that the chair won't collapse when I sit on it.") The faith must move from your mind to your heart.

The Bible says that Satan and the demons know that Jesus is the Son of God, but that factual knowledge doesn't save them. They have the knowledge in their head, but they don't have faith in their hearts. Many of the Jewish leaders who persecuted Jesus had all of the information to know that He was the Messiah. But they didn't want to put their trust in Him (see Mark 12:34).

Trust in God means that your faith has gone beyond mere intellectual knowledge of His existence. It means you are certain that His plan for you is better than your plan, and you are willing to stake your life on that trust. To follow our chair analogy, you don't just talk about the ability of the chair to hold you, you actually sit on it.

- **Will:** Knowledge and trust are both insufficient to constitute true faith unless you conform your will to what you believe. There must be some action behind your faith. Faith involves attitude and emotions and behavior. In other words, your faith should be so strong that you voluntarily conform to God's principles. Not because you are forced to, but because you have faith that God's values are best for you. And to conclude our chair analogy: You don't just sit nervously on the chair with your feet planted firmly on the ground in the event of a sudden collapse. You actually relax on the chair, maybe cross your legs, and lean back with absolutely no concern that the chair will falter (and in your euphoria, you probably drip hot sauce from the burrito onto your lap).

Despite what the Darwinists say, there is nothing irrational about faith in God. Many people, perhaps even you, are proof of that. They decide to put their faith in God after carefully and thoughtfully examining the claims of Christ and the evidence that they see in the world and in other people's lives. For most people, it is a well-thought-out, deliberate, and reasoned decision.

*C*hristian faith is not an irrational leap. Examined objectively, the claims of the Bible are rational propositions well supported by reason and evidence.

—Charles Colson

Faith Doesn't Put You on the Lunatic Fringe

Faith in God doesn't mean that you have to disconnect all the synapses in your brain. And you aren't automatically relegated to the category of "mental pygmy" in the scientific community if you are a proponent of intelligent design theory (although the Darwinists would make it appear so).

If macroevolution was the "obvious fact" that the Darwinists say it is, then you wouldn't expect to find any self-respecting scientist on the side of intelligent design, right? And with the exception of a few wackos, everyone should be believing macroevolution and rejecting intelligent design, right? And if *you* believe the intelligent design arguments, then you must be one of the wackos, right? Wrong. Wrong. Wrong.

There are thousands of scientists (some who believe in God and some who don't) who reject the notion of macroevolution:

- The respected molecular biologist Michael Denton declares: "Ultimately the Darwinian theory of evolution is no more nor less than the greatest cosmogenic myth of the twentieth century."

- The director of the zoological museum and director of research at the national Center of Scientific Research in France, Dr. Lewis Bounoure, says, "Evolution is a fairy tale for grown-ups."

From what we can determine, the number of scientists who believe in intelligent design theory is less than the number of card-carrying Darwinists. But nobody is voting, so the numbers on each side aren't really the issue. The real issue is that there are thousands of scientists who are willing to formulate their beliefs based on the evidence they see. These are not a bunch of wild-eyed radicals on the lunatic fringe of the scientific community. They are credible scholars who find the Darwinian theory to be lacking and the theory of intelligent design to be persuasive.

Of course, this is all horrific to the Darwinists. But they have an even greater secret that they want to keep from you: Not only do many scientists reject the notion of macroevolution in favor of intelligent design, but many of them also happen to believe in God. Shock! We're talking about real, live, lab-coat-wearing, telescope-gazing, microscope-peering scientists who believe in God.

In his book *Origins: The Lives and Worlds of Modern Cosmologists,* MIT professor Alan Lightman said, "Contrary to popular myths, scientists appear to have the same range of attitudes about religious matters as does the general public." That doesn't mean much unless you have the relevant data, so here is what a recent Gallup poll revealed:

- On any given Sunday, about 45 percent of all Ph.D. scientists are in church.

- For the general public, the figure is 47 percent.

So, a Ph.D. degree in science doesn't seem to make much difference in determining whether people believe in God.

With increasing frequency, scientists are publicly proclaiming their belief in God:

- Dr. Henry "Fritz" Schaefer III is the Graham Perdue Professor of Chemistry and the director of the Center for Computational Quantum Chemistry at the University of Georgia. He has been nominated for the Nobel prize and was recently cited as the third-most-quoted chemist in the world. Here is what he said about God in *U.S. News & World Report,* December 23, 1991: "The significance and joy in my science comes in the occasional moments of discovering something new and saying to myself, 'So that's how God did it!' My goal is to understand a little corner of God's plan."

- Dr. Charles Townes teaches at U.C. Berkeley. He won a little award called the Nobel prize for developing the laser (the scientific kind, not the little pen kind that the junior high kids use at the movie theater to put a little red dot on the movie screen). Dr. Townes has said, "In my view, the question of origin seems to be left unanswered if we explore from a scientific view alone. Thus, I believe there is a need for some religious or metaphysical explanation. I believe in the concept of God and in His existence."

So if you find yourself persuaded by the intelligent design theory, or if you approach your science with a belief in God, you don't need to feel like an intellectual outcast. You are in the company of a lot of brainpower.

God Requires Faith, but Darwin Does, Too

The Darwinists are correct when they say that a belief in God requires faith. It does. We don't know why God designed it that way. Let's face it, He could have made Himself so very obvious that faith wasn't required:

- Everybody could have had an imprint on their foot that reads "made by God," just like the Barbie dolls are all stamped "made by Mattel." Nobody ever wonders about Barbie's manufacturer.

- God could have arranged the cloud formations to spell out His name every day. It would be like a gigantic Power-Point presentation in the sky. Everyone would be a believer if the sky at noontime always read: "I am God and you are not."

- God could have made the animals able to sing. Now, singing animals might not be proof of the existence of God. (We have heard a few country western recordings that sounded a lot like animals in distress. When hearing such yelping, some people might wonder whether God actually exists because, hey, how could God allow such misery?) But suppose all of the animals sang hymns. A frog chorus of "How Great Thou Art" or cows mooing the lyrics and tune of "Amazing Grace" would probably convince even the most hardened skeptic.

We don't have all of the deep theological answers about why God requires faith, but we have a few thoughts about it:

- God gave enough evidence to make Himself known if we are interested in finding Him.

- God didn't create us as robots. He wants us to make up our own minds. (The theologians call it "free will.") We don't have to believe in Him if we don't want to.

- God is a perfect gentleman. He won't force Himself on us.

We find it ironic that the Darwinists are so critical of how much faith is required for belief in God, when it seems that a belief in Darwinism requires just as much faith.

Keith Stewart Thomson wrote an article for the *American Zoologist* entitled "Macroevolution: The Morphological Problem." In it he said that "[t]he basic article of faith of a gradualist approach is that major morphological innovation can be produced without some sort of saltation [the sudden appearance of a new organism]." Hmmm. He is saying that the premise of Darwinism—gradual changes from one species to another—is a "basic article of faith." In other words, it is something that has to be believed without being able to be seen. Isn't that like the definition of faith in God—believing what you can't see?

Darwinists criticize the intelligent design movement for being unscientific because it is based on unobservable objects or events (such as God or a "designer"). But Darwinism also appeals to unobservables. Stephen Meyer, a Cambridge University graduate in philosophy of science and a professor at Whitworth College, writes:

> In evolutionary science you have all kinds of unobservables. The transitional life forms that occupy the

branching-points on Darwin's tree of life have never been observed in the rock record. They've been postulated only because they help Darwinists explain the variety of life forms we observe today.

What Ya Gonna Take: Little Steps or Gigantic Leaps?

Since both intelligent design and Darwinism require an element of faith, maybe we should drop the debate and call it a draw. But wait. Maybe there is more to it than that. As we discussed above, faith shouldn't be blind. It doesn't have to be unsubstantiated. It should be based on some evidence. Shouldn't there be a difference between reasonable faith ("I have faith that the chair will support me") and irrational faith ("I just bought a new car because I have faith that this lotto ticket will win the jackpot")? Isn't there a difference between taking a small step of faith and taking a gigantic leap of faith?

Let's put intelligent design and Darwinism to the "small step" or "gigantic leap" test. Let's start with intelligent design.

Does Believing in Intelligent Design Require a Small Step of Faith or a Gigantic Leap of Faith?

Well, let's review the evidence for an intelligent designer. You can reread chapters 5 through 9 if you like, but here is an oversimplified summary:

- *The big bang.* Big bang cosmology shows that the universe had a point of beginning. It was the effect that had to have a cause.

- *The fine-tuned universe.* All of the odds point to the fact that life should be impossible anyplace in the universe. But against all odds, our planet in our solar system in our galaxy is "just right" for life. All of the variables point to the fact that there was an intelligent designer.

- *The origin of life.* Darwinism doesn't offer a legitimate explanation for how life emerged from nonliving chemicals. And the fossil record doesn't support the idea of transitional life-forms that all grew from common ancestry. The inference of an intelligent designer is overwhelming.

- **Human life.** There is no paleontological support for the idea that humans descended from the apes. The human race just showed up. How could that have happened if we were not created by an intelligent designer? The information code of DNA gives further support for created life.

Okay. You decide (after all, this book is for your benefit). Check the appropriate box.

I believe that intelligent design requires a:

❑ Small step of faith

❑ Gigantic leap of faith

Does Believing in Darwinism Require a Small Step of Faith or a Gigantic Leap of Faith?

Now let's shift to the other side of the debate and review what we know about Darwinism with another oversimplified summary:

- **The fossil record.** Darwin said the theory of macroevolution would be proven by the fossil record. But that isn't the case. In fact, just the opposite has happened. The fossil record not only doesn't support the theory, but it seems to disprove it.

We *are now about 150 years after Darwin and the knowledge of the fossil record has been greatly expanded. We now have a quarter of a million fossil species, but the situation hasn't changed much...We have even fewer examples of evolutionary transition than we had in Darwin's time.*

—David Raup

- **Random chance.** Darwin's entire theory is premised on the chance development of life. But as we reviewed in chapters 5-7, the odds are against life just appearing by chance. It is not just a matter of a long shot, like winning the lottery. The odds are so astronomical as to make it virtually impossible that life appeared anywhere in the universe by random chance.

- **Irreducible complexity.** Darwin acknowledged that his theory would be disproved if it could be determined that there was any organism that couldn't "evolve" in gradual stages. The work of biochemist Michael Behe has established the irreducible complexity of the human cell. The complicated, interrelated workings of this organism can't be reduced to a simpler stage. The cell makes Darwinism a hard sell.

It's time for you to vote again. Check the appropriate box.

I believe that Darwinism requires a:

❑ Small step of faith

❑ Gigantic leap of faith

Perhaps we haven't done a very good job of concealing our bias. (Okay. We admit that we've let our personal opinion soak through.) But honestly, we aren't trying to persuade you one way or the other. We are just trying to put the evidence on the table so you can make the analysis for yourself.

Our point is simply this: Since Darwinism itself requires faith, then it is dishonest for Darwinists to dismiss intelligent design as being "unscientific" because it requires an element of faith. And it seems that each successive scientific discovery makes faith in an intelligent designer easier and faith in Darwinism a harder stretch.

The Size of Your Faith Is Determined by Your Concept of How Big God Is

Stephen Hawking is probably the best-known contemporary scientist. His book *A Brief History of Time* was a bestseller (over 15 million copies sold). The fact that the general public would actually *read* a book about cosmology proves that it must be interesting.

A Brief History of Time focuses on Hawking's investigations of the singularity and horizons around black holes and at the beginning of time. If you haven't read the book, you might be surprised to learn that it says a lot about God. Hawking has stated, "It is difficult to discuss the beginning of the universe without mentioning the concept of God. My work on the origin of the universe is on the borderline between science and religion, but I try to stay on the scientific side of the border."

Some people have read his book and called Hawking an atheist. He strongly denies this characterization. He claims to be an agnostic or deist or something more along those lines. While he acknowledges the possibility of God, several passages in *A Brief History of Time* suggest that Hawking lacks sufficient faith for a wholehearted belief in God. Here is one of them: "We are such insignificant creatures on a minor planet of a very average star in the outer suburb of one of a hundred billion galaxies. So it is difficult to believe in a God that would care about us or even notice our existence."

Isn't it interesting how the same evidence can be viewed completely differently? Hawking looks at our existence in the universe and says, in effect, that "we are so insignificant that no God could care about us." But other scientists look at the same facts and say, in effect, that "we must be so very special to God because He went to such great lengths to create a suitable environment for us."

Maybe your faith is in direct proportion to your concept of God.

What's the Real Hang-Up?

We want to conclude this chapter by speaking personally to the skeptics—those folks who continue to reject the notion that our existence is due to the creative act of God. (The rest of you can skip ahead to the end of the chapter. Or you can read along silently, but please don't interrupt.)

To you skeptics, we want to say that we respect your right to have your own opinion. And we acknowledge that you aren't alone, because many people doubt the existence of God (although a recent Gallup poll shows that the majority of Americans believe that God was involved in the process of the origin of the world). If you don't find the evidence for intelligent design to be persuasive, we will respect your analysis. But we hope you are being honest with yourself. In other words, we ask that you make this one last gut check:

> Is your lack of faith in God the result of objective analysis of the evidence, or is your lack of faith in God based on your fear of being accountable to Him?

Many people find excuses for refusing to believe in God. We will admit that there are many perplexing issues about God (even for those who believe in Him). For example:

- If God created the world, how come there is so much evil and suffering in it?

- How is it possible that a loving God would really send people to hell for eternity?

- How come Christ claimed to be the only way to God? Why aren't other religions just as valid?

- Why do foods that are bad for you taste so good, and foods that are good for you taste so bad? (Okay, this question has nothing to do with God. We just wonder about it, and we wanted to see if you were paying attention.)

These are legitimate questions, but there are answers to them. (Chapter 11 will give you a pretty good explanation—except for the food question.) But many people still refuse to put their faith in God even when they realize the answers to these "objections." When you get down to the basic hang-up, they just don't want to be bothered with God in their life. So it is easier to deny His existence than to deal with Him.

Your lack of faith in God is your own decision. But you owe it to yourself to make sure you realize the underlying reasons for your refusal to believe in God. Is your decision based on the evidence, or is it just a stubborn attitude?

A man rejects God neither because of intellectual demands nor because of the scarcity of evidence. A man rejects God because of a moral resistance that refuses to admit his need for God.

—Ravi Zacharias

"What's That Again?"

1. Faith and science are not mutually exclusive.

2. Faith is not blind acceptance of unsubstantiated facts. Faith involves an informed decision based on available evidence.

3. If you have faith in God, you are not a part of a lunatic fringe group. Many of the leading scientists support intelligent design theory, and many of them profess a profound belief in the God of the Bible.

4. Darwinists try to dismiss intelligent design theory as being unscientific because it requires faith in a designer. But belief in Darwinism requires faith in theories that are as yet unsubstantiated.

5. The evidence for God may require a small step of faith, but belief in Darwinism may require a gigantic leap of faith.

6. If you are still skeptical about God, make sure that your lack of faith is based on an objective analysis of the evidence and not on a subconscious stubborn desire to have life your own way.

Dig Deeper

We heartily recommend *The Case for Christ: A Journalist's Personal Investigation of the Evidence for Jesus* by Lee Strobel. Strobel obtained an advanced law degree (a masters in Studies of Law) and served as a journalist and legal editor for the *Chicago Tribune*. In this bestselling book, Strobel tells the story of how he went from being an atheist to being a Christian by interviewing 13 leading experts on the historical evidence for Jesus Christ and then analyzing that information with his legal and journalistic skills. If you are skeptical about the claims of Christ, you'll love this book. Strobel was a skeptic, and he deals with the questions you probably have (since he had them himself).

A more recent book by Strobel is *The Case for Faith: A Journalist Investigates the Toughest Objections to Christianity.* All of the questions and doubts about God don't go away automatically when you take that step of faith and become a Christian. Even after becoming a Christian, Strobel had lingering questions about some of life's most perplexing issues. In this book, he identifies eight major objections to faith in God. (For example, number one is that a loving God cannot exist since evil and suffering are present in the world.) We think you'll like the style of this book. Strobel writes like an investigative reporter (because he is one).

In this chapter we've been asking what it means to have faith in God. If you want a drastic change of perspective, we suggest that you read *Creation: A Witness to the Wonder of God* by Mark D. Futato. By examining the wonders and aspects of the Creation of the world, Futato emphasizes God's faithfulness to us.

◻ ◻ ◻

Questions for Reflection and Discussion

1. How do you define *faith?*

2. Do you have a belief in God? If so, which phrase best describes your faith: (a) an unquestioning belief; or (b) a confident trust or reliance? Explain the difference.

3. Is intelligence a factor in your faith? If it is, then explain in what way.

4. Why are Darwinists so insistent that faith and intellect are mutually exclusive?

5. In what ways do *knowledge, trust,* and *will* factor into a person's faith?

6. What evidence is available that makes a belief in intelligent design a rational and reasoned decision?

7. What are some of the as-yet unproved assumptions in which the Darwinists must place their faith?

8. Do you think it takes more faith to believe in Darwinism or to believe in intelligent design? What is the basis for your answer?

Moving On...

We ended this chapter by raising some of the perplexing questions that people have about God. Maybe you have wondered about some of those issues. Many of the questions about God get resolved when you get the "big picture" of God's plan. God's blueprint for the world didn't stop after He created it. He has a plan and purpose for the world, and for you in particular, that extends for the rest of eternity.

In the last part of this book (chapters 11 and 12), we are going to focus on the big picture of God's plan. We'll look at the specifics in chapter 11. Then in chapter 12 we'll talk about how your perspectives on life are affected by whether or not you believe in God's plan. Are we getting a little offtrack from our subject of origins by looking at the future? We don't think so. Whether you realize it or not, what you believe about how life began has an effect on what you think about how it is going to end.

Part III

And God Saw That It Was Good

Chapter 11

While as yet no star traversed its course, no sun threw its flood of light and energy through space, no systems of stars and suns swept through infinity in mighty curves and uniform relations, there God was; He the eternal without beginning. He who is above the whole course of time, He who is in harmony beyond explanation possesses unity and life, the Father, the Son, and the Holy Spirit, the basis of eternity, the Living One, the only God.

—*Eric Sauer*

There's an old saying that the only sure things in life are death and taxes (Bruce is a probate lawyer, and he can confirm that). Is there anything else we can be sure of? If you were to survey a dozen different people on the subject, you would probably get a dozen different answers. Some of these answers would include the following:

- Republicans and Democrats are never going to get along.

- Parents are never going to like their kids' music.

- The Cubs will never win the World Series again.

When you are sure of something, it takes on the nature of reality for you. When you're not sure of something, it's not real to you. In other words, your reality is confined to your own experience. The problem is that your experience is confined to what your five senses can take in. If you can personally see it, taste it, smell it, hear it, and feel it, then it's real.

But what about those things above and beyond your five senses? Are they real? This is an important question, because ultimately the Creator of the universe is above and beyond your five senses. And so is His eternal plan.

God's Eternal Plan

*T*here is a scene in the groundbreaking movie *The Matrix* in which Morpheus (Laurence Fishburne), the wise leader of the ragtag rebel force (why are rebel forces always ragtag?), tries to convince Neo (Keanu Reeves) that the world he sees around him is an illusion. Morpheus offers to show Neo the truth about the real world.

"What is real?" Neo asks.

"How do you define *real?*" Morpheus answers. "If you're talking about what you can hear, what you can feel, what you can smell, what you can taste, and what you can see, then *real* is simply electrical signals interpreted by your brain. It is the world that has been pulled over your eyes to blind you to the truth."

Morpheus then shows Neo the "truth" about the real world: It's a dark, decaying, depraved world where human beings are being harvested to service beings of higher intelligence (if you think that's far-fetched, wait until you read Chapter 12).

The Wachowski brothers, who wrote and directed *The Matrix,* aren't theologians, but they captured something very profound in their film that relates directly to this chapter and the final section of this book.

In this book we've looked at the universe and how it began. We've asked questions about the galaxies and stars and planets, all of which were designed for life on this big blue marble we call "home." We have talked about how God created the earth and everything in it—including humanity—down to the most minute detail. God made everything and everyone for a purpose, and He gave each person a reason to live in the here and now. God also gave each person the freedom to choose between the Creator and the creation. We can either believe that there's something beyond the here and now, or we can believe that this world is all there is. The choice is ours.

So why doesn't everyone believe? Why do so many people refuse to exercise their faith in the reasonable and rational idea that God is there? Why do they believe the less reasonable and less rational idea that the universe is the only reality there is, and that God had nothing to do with it?

Let's go back to Morpheus's statement for a moment. If you define *real* by what you can hear, touch, smell, taste, and see—in other words, if you use just your five senses to perceive reality—then *real* to you is only what you can personally experience in the physical realm. You have confined your reality to the *natural* world. (In fact, this is a characteristic of Darwinism, sometimes called *naturalism,* which we covered in chapter 2 and will discuss again in chapter 12.)

The Reality of the Supernatural

The truth is, no one—not even the most ardent Darwinist—confines his reality to the physical world. If he did, then he would have to deny the existence of some very real things that are—

- *Intangible*—Simply put, anything you can't touch or feel is intangible. Do such things exist? Of course they do. Your emotions are intangible. You can feel the effects of your emotions (and so can other people), but you can't touch them. You can't experience your emotions with any of your five senses, yet they are there, beyond the natural world.

Then there's the whole matter of personality and essence. What is it that makes you who you are? Certainly your physical appearance is a start, but that's not the *real* you. It's hard to explain, but the real you is locked in your consciousness. Pieces of the real you come out in your personality, but there will always be parts of you that no one ever "sees."

- *Invisible*—At its simplest, *invisible* means "not capable of being seen" (intangible things are also invisible). Invisibility very clearly applies to the unseen forces of nature. Have you ever seen the wind? You see the effects of wind, but you can't actually see wind. Creatures in the natural world also possess invisible qualities. Philip Yancey describes an ability that every creature on Earth possesses, "a way to connect to the environment around it, a means to pick up and process what is out there."

There is an invisible mechanism that enables "blind" bats to detect tiny insects, pigeons to find their way home, and dogs to hear and smell things far beyond human capabilities. These invisible qualities aren't part of our physical world, yet they are real.

I must assume that my senses never furnish a complete representation of another person. I can learn a lot about you through watching you, listening to you, touching you. Yet there always remains a part of you inaccessible to me, the person inside your body, the real "you."

—Philip Yancey

- *Infinite*—The universe itself is finite, and therefore the natural world is finite. Yet there are things within our world that are infinite, without limits, endless. Here's an example from mathematics, which is considered a "hard" science. The ratio of the circumference of any circle to its diameter is approximately 22:7. This ratio is also known as "pi" (not the Marie Callender variety), and the answer is always 3.14159+. The "plus" sign means that the number keeps going infinitely. Computers have taken pi to more than 200 billion decimal places, but the number keeps going. The decimal places go on infinitely without repeating or ending in a zero.

Things that are intangible, invisible, and infinite—which you could lump together and call supernatural—exist above and beyond our natural world.

---

*S*upernatural—*above and beyond what is natural.*

Longing for the Supernatural

Our culture is dominated by naturalism, a philosophy which denies the existence of the supernatural. Yet we know that the supernatural exists in the ways we just described. Beyond the existence of the supernatural in things in the natural world, we also know that the supernatural exists in the spiritual world, even if people try to deny its existence. Dr. Hugh Ross puts it this way: "All human beings—men, women, and children, in all geographical and historical contexts—possess innate knowledge not instilled by human instruction but by our Creator. Whether our family and culture affirm these beliefs or deny them, humans gradually become aware of these things."

Dr. Ross goes on to point out two of these "innate truths" that the Creator has placed in every human being:

- *The truth about God.* "For the truth about God is known to them instinctively. God has put this knowledge in their hearts" (Romans 1:19).

- *The truth about eternity.* "He has planted eternity in the human heart" (Ecclesiastes 3:11).

Our Supernatural Culture

Our popular culture is laced with books, television shows, music, movies, and Web sites devoted to the supernatural. Beyond the entertainment industry, private individuals continue to fund the ongoing SETI (Search for Extra-Terrestrial Intelligence) program in the hope of finding intelligent life above and beyond our own.

Looking for Eternal Life in All the Wrong Places

As human beings who are created by God in His own image, we can't help but think about God and things above and beyond ourselves. It's part of our genetic makeup. Not only is the truth right there in front of us, it's also right here *inside us*. So why doesn't everyone accept this truth? Because our loving Creator has given us a choice. He may have programmed the truth chip inside our beings, but He didn't program us to automatically say yes. God gave us the freedom and the ability to choose what's right and what's wrong. The problem is that many people have chosen to believe things that go against their innate knowledge.

> *Instead of believing what they knew was the truth about God, they deliberately chose to believe lies. So they worshiped the things God made but not the Creator himself, who is to be praised forever. Amen* (Romans 1:25).

There's a reason why people are reluctant to accept the existence of a personal, intelligent designer. It's not that they are less intelligent than everyone else (in fact, many times they seem *more* intelligent). They are simply making a choice according to the freedom that God gave them. If they haven't yet chosen God, what are they choosing? Like the Bible says, they are choosing "the things God made but not the Creator himself." Even though God's creation can never substitute for God, you can see why people put the created world in place of God. Yet our experience has shown (and the Bible says) that regardless of the choice, people still have this longing for something beyond this world and beyond themselves. They want to know if the truth is "out there."

A Brief History of Eternity

At the end of his book *A Brief History of Time*, Stephen Hawking writes, "If we should discover a complete theory...we shall...be able to take part in the discussion of the question of why it is that we and the Universe exist. If we find the answer to that it will be the ultimate triumph of human reason—for then we will know the mind of God."

Isn't that what humankind has tried to do since time began? As curious and self-willed people, we have always wanted to know what God knows. When Satan came to Adam and Eve in God's perfect garden, here's what he said would happen if the first couple disobeyed God:

> *You will become just like God, knowing everything, both good and evil* (Genesis 3:5).

Just as that little lie (with its big consequences) appealed to Adam and Eve, it has appealed to every person since. Even when people deny God exists, they want to be like Him! They want to know what God knows, and they want to be what God is.

But all we have is our five senses. We can't detect God's existence or His presence by subjecting Him to natural laws. Furthermore, we live in the four dimensions of length, width, height, and time. God doesn't exist within the confines of these dimensions, just as He does not live within the scope of our senses. He is above and beyond. As the prophet Isaiah wrote, God is "the high and lofty one who inhabits eternity" (Isaiah 57:15). He is "the one who is, who always was, and who is still to come" (Revelation 1:4).

> *Before the mountains were created, before you made the earth and the world, you are God, without beginning or end* (Psalm 90:2).

The Extra-Dimensionality of God

That God exists outside our four dimensions of length, width, height, and time is not improbable. Science has proven that extra dimensions exist. Einstein's theory of general relativity showed that the universe had a singular, finite beginning, and it operates within a singular boundary, not only for matter and energy but also for space and time. This means that the cause (or Causer) of the universe must exist outside our dimensions in order for the effect (or universe) to exist. Hugh Ross writes, "Physicists can now demonstrate that the Causer exists and operates in several spatial dimensions beyond our three, as well as in at least one more time dimension (or the equivalent)."

God Is Incomprehensible

The eternity of God is one of His characteristics, and only God is eternal. When God created the universe, He created the physical laws that govern the heavens and the earth. He designed the four dimensions and our five senses so we could function as human beings and enjoy God's creation. He created us with an innate sense of eternity (Ecclesiastes 3:11), but He did not create us as eternal beings. Unlike God, we have a beginning. Unlike God, we are finite.

There's a downside to our confinement in time as it relates to God's existence in eternity. As R. C. Sproul writes, "The finite cannot grasp (or contain) the infinite." We can't put God in a box. We can't figure Him out. Theologians refer to this as the "incomprehensibility" of God. We'll never be able to fully understand Him. Not only that, writes Wayne Grudem, but we can never fully understand any single characteristic of God, such as—

- **His greatness.** "His greatness is beyond discovery!" (Psalm 145:3).

- **His understanding.** "His understanding is beyond comprehension!" (Psalm 147:5).

- **His knowledge.** "Such knowledge is too wonderful for me, too great for me to know!" (Psalm 139:6).

- **His ways.** "How impossible it is for us to understand his decisions and his methods!" (Romans 11:33).

In the ancient world, one of Job's friends had this to say about the incomprehensibility of God:

> *Can you solve the mysteries of God? Can you discover everything there is to know about the Almighty? Such knowledge is higher than the heavens—but who are you? It is deeper than the underworld—what can you know in comparison to him? It is broader than the earth and wider than the sea* (Job 11:7-10).

You could do one of three things in response to this incomprehensible God:

1. Come up with your own "unknown god," like the Athenians in Acts 17. (Your unknown god doesn't have to be an actual idol or statue. It could be some sort of mixture of different religions and spiritual ideas.)

2. Ignore God altogether and put your faith in nature.

3. Accept that God is incomprehensible, but believe that He is knowable.

God Is Knowable

We like the third option. Even though God is incomprehensible—meaning that He cannot be fully understood—we can know certain things about Him. How can that be? Because God has given us information about Himself through the Bible, His personal message to us. Grudem writes that the Bible tells us these things about God and much more:

- *He is love.* "But anyone who does not love does not know God—for God is love" (1 John 4:8).

- *He is light.* "This is the message he has given us to announce to you: God is light and there is no darkness in him at all" (1 John 1:5).

- *He is Spirit.* "For God is Spirit, so those who worship him must worship in spirit and in truth" (John 4:24).

- *He is fair and just.* "And he is entirely fair and just in this present time when he declares sinners to be right in his sight because they believe in Jesus" (Romans 3:26).

We don't have to know everything about God to know God. Because we have the Bible, we have *true* knowledge of God, even if it isn't *full* knowledge. When the Bible says that God's thoughts are "completely different" from our thoughts (Isaiah 55:8), it doesn't mean we can never know what God is thinking. David wrote, "How precious are your thoughts about me, O God! They are innumerable!" (Psalm 139:17).

Open Your Eyes

The Matrix has nothing on the Bible when it comes to drama. How's this for a movie plot:

Movie Treatment for

Elisha and the Chariots of Fire

Based on 2 Kings 6:8-23

The king of Aram and the king of Israel are at war, but the Israeli forces are winning because someone is tipping off the king of Israel as to the secret location of the Aramean army. The king of Aram is convinced there is a traitor among his ranks, but his soldiers assure him that the true culprit is the prophet Elisha, who is no spy, but a "man of God." The king of Aram assembles "a great army with many chariots and horses to surround the city" where Elisha is staying. It looks like curtains for our hero.

In the morning Elisha's servant goes to the edge of the city and sees the vast army ready to capture his master.

Servant (shaking): "What will we do now?"

Elisha (confident): "Don't be afraid! For there are more on our side than on theirs!"

The servant looks around and sees nothing. Has his master gone mad? Then the man of God prays to God on behalf of his servant, asking God to "open his eyes and let him see!" Then the Lord opens the servant's eyes, and when he looks up, he sees the hillside around Elisha filled with horses and "chariots of fire."

If you want to see how the movie ends, check out the passage of Scripture. But you already know what happens. The enemy army is defeated because God defends His man and His nation. The king of Aram may have a huge natural army, but Elisha has a vastly superior supernatural army unseen to the natural eye.

This is the reality of the *real* world. Just the opposite of *The Matrix*, the world we see around us is the world that is decaying. The unseen world where God and His heavenly host dwell is the real world. Our natural eyes can't see this world. Like Elisha's servant, we see only the world around us with its dangers and difficulties. If we would just open our eyes to the things of God, we would see wonders far greater than we could ever imagine:

No eye has seen, no ear has heard, and no mind has imagined what God has prepared for those who love him (1 Corinthians 2:9).

The Christian Mind

Even though we can never fully comprehend God, we can know Him. And even though we can't possibly imagine what God has prepared for those who love and follow Him, we can get a glimpse of eternity and a look at God's ways:

But we know these things because God has revealed them to us by his Spirit, and his Spirit searches out everything and shows us even God's deep secrets (1 Corinthians 2:10).

If this is getting into a weird area for you, that's okay. The Bible is very clear that "God's ways seem foolish" to those who don't believe God and His message "because they want a sign from heaven to prove it is true" (1 Corinthians 1:22). They want God to invade their here-and-now reality with verifiable evidence that He exists (at the very least, they want proof that alien life once visited this planet). The truth is, God has already given us a sign. Alien life has already visited this planet. (Keep reading and we'll tell you how.)

If you're not a Christian, then you have a *natural orientation.* It's difficult if not impossible for you to understand the truth about God (1 Corinthians 2:14). You have a secular mind that sees things from a temporal perspective. But if you are a Christian, then you have a *supernatural orientation.* You have a Christian mind that sees things from an eternal perspective.

Harry Blamires, a student of C. S. Lewis, wrote this about the Christian mind:

The Christian mind sees human life and human history held in the hands of God. It sees the whole universe sustained by his power and his love. It sees the natural order as dependent upon the supernatural order, time as contained within eternity. It sees this life as an inconclusive experience, preparing us for another; this world as a temporary place of refuge, not our true and final home.

The secularist is "rooted" in this world and ignores the reality beyond it; the Christian is aware of the world beyond. For the secularist, this world is the only basis of truth and knowledge; for the Christian, truth and knowledge include this world, but go beyond it as well. Jesus said that happiness and well-being come "if you live for him and make the kingdom of God your primary concern" (Matthew 6:33).

"For the Christian mind earthly well-being is not the *summum bonum,* as pain and death are not the worst evil," writes Blamires. "Eternal well-being is the final aim and end of things here. This means that success and prosperity within the earthly set-up cannot be regarded as a final criterion. Nor indeed can happiness within time be regarded as a final criterion."

God's Eternal Plan

Just as God is incomprehensible but knowable, His eternal plan for the universe and humankind is hard to understand but knowable. We're going to do the best we can to outline it for you (with a little help from Eric Sauer).

1. God's eternal plan originated from God Himself as the Creator of the universe. He is the Source of everything that exists outside Himself (Acts 17:24,28).

2. Not only does everything come from God, but everything exists by His power and for His glory (Romans 11:36).

3. God chose to create the heavens and the earth—"the things we can see and the things we can't see"—through Jesus Christ, His Son, who existed "before everything else began" (Colossians 1:16-17).

4. This has been God's purpose "from all eternity" (Ephesians 3:11). His entire plan has always centered on Christ (Ephesians 1:9).

Why Do Pain and Death Exist?

One of the most difficult questions we face is this: If God created the world, how come there is so much evil, pain, and suffering? Why does death exist? If God is so powerful, and if He is so involved in our world, why does it seem as if He is either powerless or unwilling to do anything about evil and suffering?

The Bible makes it clear that God did not create the world the way it is now. Evil, suffering, and death came about because of the disobedience and selfishness of humankind. By His very nature, God is a God of love, and He created humanity to love and glorify Him. But He did not create a race of beings who could do nothing but love Him. He created us with the freedom to choose between the benefits of His love and the consequences of sin.

God is not evil, nor did He create evil. As our representatives, Adam and Eve, the first humans, chose sin over God, thereby infecting the entire human race (Romans 5:12). Although evil, suffering, pain, and death are present and very real, they are not here for good. In God's eternal plan there is a new world coming where "there will be no more death or sorrow or crying or pain" (Revelation 21:4).

5. The reason God called everything into existence through His Son was that, from eternity, God foresaw that sin would interrupt (but not destroy) His plan. Long before the world began, God chose Jesus Christ to be the "sinless, spotless Lamb of God" so He could pay the penalty for our sin. Jesus was God's ransom for our salvation (1 Peter 1:18-20).

6. Planet Earth is the stage for the grand universal drama of the battle between God and Satan, between humankind and sin, and between good and evil. God chose to enter our four dimensions, and He chose to interact with our five senses through the Person of Jesus Christ, who is "God with us" (John 1:14).

7. It is on the earth that Jesus died on the cross for our sins, and it is on earth where Christ will finally and forever defeat the forces of evil and the finality of death so that whoever believes in Him can have eternal life (John 3:16).

Accessing God's Plan Through Faith

In chapter 10 we explained that belief and trust in God means that your faith has gone beyond just an intellectual knowledge of His existence. It means you believe that His plan for you is better than your plan, and you are willing to build your life on that belief. Your knowledge of the evidence of God's existence will only take you so far. Knowing that God exists won't save you from the penalty of sin. Neither will believing that He created the universe. As the Bible says, every person knows these things, though some suppress the truth (Romans 1:18-20).

The truth is, God has declared the entire human race guilty because of sin: "For all have sinned; all fall short of God's glorious standard" (Romans 3:23).

There is a consequence for our sin and our guilt: "For the wages of sin is death" (Romans 6:23).

But God has made it possible through His eternal plan for us to escape the death penalty:

> Yet now God in his gracious kindness declares us not guilty. He has done this through Christ Jesus, who has freed us by taking away our sins. For God sent Jesus to take the punishment for our sins and to satisfy God's anger against us. We are made right with God when we believe that Jesus shed his blood, sacrificing his life for us (Romans 3:24-25).

Why Is Jesus the Only Way?

Not only does the Bible make it clear that Jesus is the only way to get to God (Acts 4:12; 1 Timothy 2:5), but Jesus Himself said it (John 14:6). You might ask, "How can anyone be so arrogant? Aren't there many ways to God, with Jesus being just one of them?" The answer is pretty simple. Jesus is God with skin on. He is God in the flesh. Jesus was God's way of becoming human so that He could enter the world and live among us (John 1:14). But Jesus didn't come to earth to hang out, live for a while, and return to heaven. He was born to die.

The Bible says that "when we were utterly helpless, Christ came at just the right time and died for us sinners" (Romans 5:6). Jesus died in order to satisfy the judgment of God against the human race because of sin. He died in our place so we could be made right in God's sight (Romans 5:9). Jesus is the only way to God because "God was in Christ, reconciling the world to himself, no longer counting people's sins against them" (2 Corinthians 5:19). God wasn't in Buddha, or Mohammed, or Confucius, or nature. God was in Jesus Christ and Jesus Christ alone.

So you see, it's not enough to believe God exists. We must believe in what He says. We must believe in His eternal plan, which centers on the Person and work of Jesus Christ.

Accepting God's Eternal Plan Through Faith

It's one thing to know about God's eternal plan, and quite another to accept it. This is where so many people get stuck. They believe in God, they even believe that the only way to salvation is through Jesus Christ, but they can't get past the fact that there's nothing they can do to earn their salvation. They want a ticket to heaven, but they want to be able to pay for it.

Here is what separates the Christian belief system from every other belief system in the world. In every other religion, you earn your way to heaven or the afterlife by the good deeds you do, like a Boy Scout collecting merit badges. With God's eternal plan, there is no earning. Salvation is a free gift:

> *The free gift of God is eternal life through Christ Jesus our Lord* (Romans 6:23).

And there's nothing we can do to earn it:

> *God saved you by his special favor when you believed. And you can't take credit for this; it is a gift from God. Salvation is not a reward for the good things we have done, so none of us can boast about it* (Ephesians 2:8-9).

Understanding Why

Why did God set up His eternal plan this way? It's hard to understand. In many ways God's eternal plan defies all logic. But on another, deeper level, it all makes perfect sense, since God based His plan on something much greater than logic. He based His plan on love. Faith is a requirement for salvation (Ephesians 2:8-9), and our faith gives us hope (Hebrews 11:1). But the love of God is greater than faith and hope.

> *There are three things that will endure—faith, hope, and love—and the greatest of these is love* (1 Corinthians 13:13).

---

*S*o What Do I Do?

Accepting God's free gift of salvation through Jesus Christ is the most important thing you will ever do. When you are ready, here are six simple steps to follow:

1. God loves you and wants to have a personal relationship with you (John 3:16).

2. You will never satisfy God's perfect standard (Romans 3:23).

3. God sent Jesus to satisfy His standard for us (Romans 5:8).

4. Jesus is the only way to have a personal relationship with God (John 14:6).

5. Jesus is knocking at the door of your heart (Revelation 3:20).

6. You need to personally receive Jesus Christ into your life (Romans 10:9).

When you are ready, here is a simple prayer you might want to pray:

Lord Jesus, thank You for dying on the cross for my sins. I want to know You personally and live with You forever. I'm tired of running my own life. Please come into my heart. I ask You to take over. I receive You as Lord and Savior of my life. Thank You for forgiving my sins. From this day forward, make me the kind of person You want me to be. Help me to live for You for the rest of my life. I can't wait to spend eternity with You. Thank You, Jesus.

The Divine Conspiracy

Accepting God's free gift of salvation through Jesus Christ is the only way to avoid God's eternal death penalty, but it is much more than fire insurance. You don't have to wait until the end of the world (or the end of your life) to enjoy the benefits of being a Christian. Your new life in Christ begins the moment you receive Him into your life:

> *What this means is that those who become Christians become new persons. They are not the same anymore, for the old life is gone. A new life has begun!* (2 Corinthians 5:17).

In his powerful book *The Divine Conspiracy*, Dallas Willard wrote that entering into a life with Jesus Christ is not merely accepting something that happened in the past (when Jesus came to earth to die on the cross) so that we can have a secure future (when Jesus comes back to earth again). "Jesus offers himself as God's doorway into the life that is truly life. Confidence in him leads us today, as in other times, to become his apprentices in eternal living."

Jesus satisfies our hunger for significance, which God planted in every human being. All of us want to count for something. We want to find meaning somewhere outside ourselves. "We are, all of us, never-ceasing spiritual beings with a unique eternal calling to count for good in God's great universe," Willard writes. The only way for that to happen is to access and accept God's eternal plan, "so that we can do the good things he planned for us long ago" (Ephesians 2:10).

---

*J*esus came among us to show and teach the life for which we were made. He came very gently, opened access to the governance of God with him, and set afoot a conspiracy of freedom in truth among human beings. Having overcome death he remains among us. By relying on his word and presence we are enabled to reintegrate the little realm that makes up our life into the infinite rule of God. And that is the eternal kind of life. Caught up in his active rule, our deeds become an element in God's eternal history. They are what God and we do together, making us part of his life and him a part of ours.

—Dallas Willard

"What's That Again?"

1. God has given each person the freedom to choose between the Creator and the creation.

2. Our culture is dominated by naturalism, which denies the existence of the supernatural. But there is plenty of evidence that the supernatural exists.

3. Because God is incomprehensible, some people come up with their own "unknown god," while others ignore God and put their faith in nature.

4. Because God is knowable through the Bible, His personal message to humankind, we can know all about His eternal plan.

5. God's eternal plan is centered on the Person and work of Jesus Christ.

6. You must access and accept God's eternal plan by faith.

7. When you do, you become a part of God's eternal plan, which secures for you life in the future while giving your life significance now.

God's great conspiracy of bringing people to Himself through the Person and work of Jesus stretches from eternity to eternity, but you can be a part of it now, while you live on Earth. Your life can take on meaning and significance as you allow the power of God to work through you each and every day of your life.

Dig Deeper

The Christian Mind by Harry Blamires is an older book, but you can still find it, which we suggest you do. Blamires will challenge you to think with a supernatural orientation. Don't believe for a minute that supernatural thinking will put your head in the clouds. The only way to impact culture is to bring the presence of God into it through the thoughts and the deeds of thinking Christians.

Dallas Willard teaches philosophy at the University of Southern California, and he is one of the most original Christian thinkers of our time. We highly recommend *The Divine Conspiracy,* in which Dr. Willard shows the relevance of God to every aspect of our existence.

We said we were going to work in all of Dr. Hugh Ross's books, so here's one more: *Beyond the Cosmos.* This is where Dr. Ross explores the extra-dimensionality of God as shown through astronomy and physics.

◻ ◻ ◻

*Q*uestions for *R*eflection and *D*iscussion

1. Name three additional intangible realities of our world. Name three additional invisible realities of our world. Name three additional infinite realities of our world.

2. How is it possible that a culture rooted in naturalism is so obsessed with the supernatural? Why do so many people who are interested in the supernatural choose to orient their worldview around naturalism rather than theism?

3. Why is it important that God is both incomprehensible and knowable? Explain the difference between comprehending and knowing something.

4. Does the incomprehensibility of God comfort you, or does it bother you? What practical things can you do to know God better?

5. Why is God's eternal plan for the universe and humankind so hard for some people to believe and accept? Is it possible to believe this plan and not accept it? Give an example.

6. Explain why you do or don't agree with this statement: "Christianity is the only belief system where you cannot earn your way to salvation by your good deeds."

7. Explain why God decided to center His plan for restoring humankind and the universe on the person and work of Jesus. Could God have accomplished the same thing without sending Jesus to earth? Why or why not?

◻ ◻ ◻

Moving On...

We digressed from the whole issue of origins for one chapter so that you would have an opportunity to step back and think about the choices in front of you. When you study how it all began, you ultimately have to come face-to-face with the implications of what it all means and the difference it's going to make in the way you live.

That's what the next (and final) chapter is all about. What do you do with what you know? Can your knowledge and beliefs make any difference in how you live and how you view the world around you?

Chapter 12

It can be argued on the basis of facts concerning the nature of man and the conditions of human life that human beings have a deep-seated need to form some general picture of the total universe in which they live, in order to be able to relate their own fragmentary activities to the universe as a whole in a way meaningful to them; and that a life in which this is not carried through is a life impoverished in a most significant respect.

—W. P. Alston

As we embark with you on the last chapter of this book, we want to reinforce the importance of the origins debate. We wouldn't want you to finish this book with the feeling that the subject of origins is a debate that affects the scientists but has no relevance for you in your everyday life. Don't think that it doesn't really matter to you—because it does!

This is, in fact, the most important chapter of the entire book. (We might have said that earlier about the other chapters, but this time we *really* mean it.) The facts and figures about outer space, fossils, and DNA are interesting, but your life will be the same whether you remember them or not. This chapter is different because it raises an issue that impacts your life right now and into the future. In fact, it is so important, we can't wait until the chapter officially starts before we say how critical it is, so here it is: What you decide about creation and evolution affects how you live your life.

It really does. And we'll explain how that can happen to you without you even realizing it (sort of like the way you find yourself humming the jingle from a commercial for a toilet bowl cleaner that you saw on television the previous night).

Deciding whether you believe in intelligent design (God) or Darwinism (no God) is the first step toward making very important decisions about your life and your future. Watch that first step. It's a doozy.

Your Life Depends on
What You Decide

*I*n the last 11 chapters, we have been talking about stuff that is so ancient that it might seem far removed from your life. Whether it was the beginning of the universe 15 billion years ago (give or take a few days), or the first human life on the planet (somewhere between 10,000 to 24,000 years ago), all of that may just seem like ancient history. But just because it is ancient doesn't mean that it isn't relevant. Let us put it into a contemporary context for you. Let's go back and start with the twentieth century. (That ought to be contemporary enough for you. We don't care how young you are—our guess is that you were living back then.)

- The twentieth century has been described as the century of physics. It was in that century that we (humans, not Bruce & Stan) learned to split the atom and turn silicon into computing power. (The impetus for the innovations of the twentieth century actually began in 1897 with the discovery of the electron, but things didn't really start kicking until the 1900s.)

The twenty-first century is predicted to be the century of biotechnology. The spark was ignited in 1953 when American biochemist James Watson and British biophysicist Francis Crick announced their discovery of the double-helix structure of the DNA molecule that carries the genetic code. Now, in the twenty-first century, the scientific community and the rest of the world stand just a few years away from the most explosive breakthrough of all time: deciphering the human genome—the 100,000 genes encoded by three billion chemical pairs in our DNA.

Now we're getting relevant to your life. We can't get much more pertinent than talking about your DNA, which determined your gender, eye color, intelligence, creativity, health, longevity, and the average length of your nostril hairs.

With each biotechnological discovery, our society is presented with ethical dilemmas. Cloning is a good example. Should it be pursued, or should science stop cloning around? From a strictly scientific standpoint, it might seem like the next natural step in biotechnological advancement. But what happens when science wants to move from cloning sheep to cloning shepherds? Think about the moral ramifications of:

- developing a class of "drones" to handle the grunt work of society

- deciding who the parents are of a clone produced in a laboratory (the donor of the genetic material, the donor of the egg into which the genetic material is transferred, or the scientist who manipulates the cells)

- raising clones as "organ donors" for the sole purpose of "harvesting" their good organs to replace the defective ones in noncloned humans

And cloning isn't the only biotechnological advancement of the twenty-first century that raises ethical issues. As medical science develops, we are faced with the continuing cultural issues of:

- abortion

- euthanasia

- genetic engineering

Are you getting the idea that you are living in a century that is going to raise moral and ethical issues that are not easily resolved? (If you don't realize it now, you will soon enough—just as soon as you wake up and smell the Starbucks.)

So how do the ethical issues of the twenty-first century relate to the beginnings of the universe 15 billion years ago? We're glad you asked. Here is the connection: What you decide about the origin of the universe will influence what you think about the ethical issues in your life.

And not just the ethical issues. What you decide about origins will influence what you think about how the world is going to end (to be more personal about it, "what is going to happen when you die"—which is basically the end of the world as far as you are concerned).

If we are correct about this, then the great origins debate becomes pretty relevant, doesn't it? If we are right, then you can't dismiss it as being theoretical or irrelevant to your situation. All of a sudden it takes on personal, intimate, and practical dimensions.

Maybe you are skeptical about whether or not we're right about this. We don't blame you. It can sneak up on you without you ever realizing it. It starts rather innocuously, with whichever Creation story you believe, and then it becomes a personal philosophy, and then that philosophy becomes your personal worldview. But you don't have to take our word for it. Allow us to explain it, and then you can decide for yourself whether what you believe about how life began influences the decisions you make in your own life.

Two Creation Stories

Sometimes people get confused with the real issues in the great origins debate. You've almost finished this book, so we know this couldn't happen to you. But those who are deprived and less fortunate than you (meaning those who haven't read this book) are likely to think that the debate is:

- God versus Darwin (but it's not)

- The Bible versus evolution (but it's not)

- Religion versus science (but it's not that either)

Boiled down to its basics, the great origins debate is about God versus no God. (This may be news to the uninitiated, but you've known this all along—or at least since chapter 3.) But we can simplify it even further. The great origins debate is really about the Creation story. Fundamentally, there are just two versions of Creation. The Bible tells one story, and the Darwinists tell another. The debate is over which story you should believe.

The Bible's Story of Creation

The Bible's story of Creation begins with God as a preexisting superintelligence. God exists in another dimension, and He brought the universe, nature, and man into existence out of nothing. He did it by simply speaking His Word, and matter responded to His command.

The point of the Bible's story of Creation is that it was planned, initiated, and sustained by God. It is a process that required His intelligence and guidance. Because humans are a part of that process, then there is a purpose to our existence. We are part of the plan. And we are accountable to God because He is in charge of it all.

---

*D*arwinism is the creation story for our culture. It tells us how we came into existence and how we relate to ultimate reality. The message of Darwinism is that we are not created by a purposeful being—God, in a word—who brought about our existence for a purpose. Instead, we and all other living things are the products of a mindless, material evolutionary process. That's the important thing about the process; it's mindless and material.

—Phillip Johnson

The Darwinist's Story of Creation

The Darwinist's story of Creation is in stark contrast to the Bible's story. The Darwinist begins the story of Creation with matter swirling around in random, undirected motion. There is nature, but that is all there is. Nature began the process of Creation all by itself through impersonal, blind, purposeless chance.

Humans are part of the Darwinist's Creation story, too. But we aren't an intentional part of it. We are just an unplanned cosmic accident. There is no reason for us being here. It just happened. Accordingly, we aren't accountable to anyone because no one is responsible for our existence.

When Science Becomes Philosophy

For centuries, the Bible's story of Creation prevailed in our culture. But then Darwin postulated his scientific theory of evolution, and the culture slowly began to shift to his way of thinking—a way that excluded any notion of God. And this shift took the theory out of the science lab and brought it into the culture as a philosophy.

When we say "philosophy," we aren't talking about an ivory tower, sitting-in-the-lotus-position, contemplating-your-belly-button type of philosophy. We're talking about a real-life, it-makes-a-difference-how-you-live kind of philosophy.

Darwin wasn't the only one responsible for this shift in cultural philosophy. There were several influential thinkers responsible for the transition: Neitzsche, Darwin, Marx, and Freud.

- Neitzsche proclaimed the death of God.

- Darwin supplied the murder weapon.

- Marx was the architect of the social consequences.

- Freud played mind games and told us what to think about ourselves.

Intellectual historians agree that these were the dominant figures of twentieth-century materialism, and the twentieth century saw us working out all the implications of these basic ideas.

Naturalism: It's All About Nothing

The "no God" philosophy is known as naturalism. Naturalism is the philosophy that nature is the only "force" in the universe, and that it is an impersonal force that acts randomly and without plan or purpose. (Sometimes the philosophy of naturalism is referred to as materialism, but don't confuse that with the desire to accumulate material possessions and wealth. Think of materialism in the philosophical sense as a universe in which matter is all that matters.)

As you read chapters 5–9, you might have wondered why Darwinism has survived as a scientific theory when there is little evidence to support it. Well, the answer is simple. Darwinism has gone way beyond a modest (and poorly supported) scientific theory. It has become a very popular and grand philosophy—a philosophy that attempts to explain the world in strictly naturalistic terms. Phillip Johnson, the law professor and analytical critic of Darwinism, says, "The whole point of Darwinism is to explain the world in a way that excludes any role for a Creator. What is being sold in the name of science is a completely naturalistic understanding of reality."

Darwinism won't be quickly dismissed as scientific theory as long as it is taken for granted as a philosophy. Darwinists readily admit that their scientific theory has become a philosophy. And they admit that they adhere to the naturalistic philosophy because they do not want to acknowledge the existence of God. A leading Darwinist, Richard Lewontin, revealed his bias as a scientist when he said, "We believe in this evolutionary theory and similar scientific concepts because we [that is, the dominant scientific faction] have an *a priori* commitment to materialism as a philosophy. That commitment must be absolute because we cannot allow a divine foot in the door."

The scientific community is devoted to naturalism as its starting point. Because they intentionally refuse to consider God's existence, they won't even consider intelligent design as a possible theory. If it flies in the face of their philosophy, they won't allow it in the laboratory.

Although naturalism is so widespread, most people do not realize that the naturalistic view of reality has its foundation in Darwinism. But the scientists do. That's why Darwinist scientists are fighting so hard to quash the revolt of the proponents of intelligent design. But as you saw in chapters 5–10, the Darwinist viewpoint isn't a slam dunk. In fact, an objective referee might call a "foul" on the Darwinist team, or maybe call them for "goal tending" or some other offense—whatever translates into basketball lingo—for their lack of sufficient supporting evidence. (We wish we could make this basketball analogy work better, but basketball isn't our sport. We should have stuck with a sport that we know, like curling, but then you wouldn't have understood the reference. We only engage in obscure sports that no one else participates in. That way we look pretty good since there is no one to compare us to.)

The Darwinists can't resort to scientific evidence to prevail in a debate with the intelligent-design proponents. They haven't shown that natural selection can create new species, the fossil record doesn't support their theory, and neither does the molecular evidence. So, to preserve naturalism as a ruling philosophy for all aspects of life (and to remove God as the basis of rationality and human existence), the Darwinists have resorted to heavy-handed methods rather than objective analysis. As Paul Feyerabend puts it:

> Scientists are not content with running their own playpens in accordance with what they regard as the rules of the scientific method; they want to universalize those rules, they want them to become part of society at large, and they use every means at their disposal—argument, propaganda, pressure tactics, intimidation, lobbying—to achieve their aims.

With these tactics, they have been successful in imposing a naturalistic philosophy on the entire culture for the last 120 years.

So What Happened to God?

Although the intelligent-design proponents are chipping away at the scientific underpinnings of Darwinism, the philosophy of naturalism remains predominant in society. That doesn't mean that God has completely disappeared from society. He is still around. But in the philosophy of naturalism, God is seen as an invention of our own minds. Here's how it all plays out:

- When evolution (macroevolution) is taught as a fact, then we are teaching naturalism as a fact (even though that philosophical perspective is not articulated).

- If the evolutionary process is our creator, then God isn't the Creator.

- With naturalism as our adopted philosophy, we have no place for God at all.

"Wait a minute!" you say. "How can the philosophy of naturalism dispense with God when so many people believe in Him?" (The Gallup polls indicated that most Americans believe in God.) Well, the Darwinists have an answer for that, and it goes something like this:

- Humans evolved as part of the unguided, random process of evolution.

- Until the arrival of enlightened thinkers like Darwin, humans didn't understand the concept of evolution. It was beyond their intellectual understanding.

- To explain their existence, these unenlightened humans created the concept of a divine being to explain how they came into being.

- So according to the naturalistic way of thinking, God did not create us. Instead, we created God.

Imagine that. Primitive human beings, lacking scientific knowledge of their true creator (evolution), concocted the notion of a grandfather-type figure in the sky. They projected certain qualities onto him. (They considered him benevolent in some respects—like a celestial Santa Claus. In other respects, he was vengeful—like a cosmic killjoy, looking to stomp on anyone who was having a good time "sinning.")

So according to the philosophy of naturalism, God doesn't really exist. If you want to believe in Him, that's okay, but He's really just a figment of your imagination. And...

- If God doesn't exist, then neither does His moral authority.

- Morality is simply a human invention.

If God is dead, then we aren't feeling so well ourselves.

—Bruce & Stan

- "Moral behavior" is whatever people agree on, and of course they can change that agreement at any time. Therefore, morality can evolve, just like everything else.

Naturalism goes further: Since everything simply evolved in a random, undirected process without a plan, purpose, or designer, then there is no absolute truth:

- Since there is no absolute morality or truth, everything is relative. Everything depends on the circumstances. Situational ethics are the order of the day. Tolerance is required for all viewpoints because each person gets to decide what is "right" for him or her.

- Of course, relativism doesn't apply in situations that involve political correctness. In these areas, certain behavior can be insisted upon.

- But political correctness can only be enforced by power because it isn't really absolutely true either (since there is no truth).

Thus the philosophy of naturalism inevitably leads to a situation in which power governs truth. Truth is what the people in power say it is. (We find it ironic that the Darwinists promote a philosophy of naturalism that says there is no truth. Yet they reject intelligent design because it contradicts the "truth" of naturalism. Hmm...)

How Philosophy Becomes a Worldview

When philosophy gets applied to the stark realities and issues of everyday life, it becomes your worldview. A worldview is the conceptual framework by which you consciously or unconsciously interpret the world around you according to your philosophical beliefs. Think of your personal philosophies as train tracks that have no switches. Your worldview is the train that travels down those tracks, in a path that is already predetermined by what you believe.

---

*M*aterialism gave us a theory which explained everything else in the whole universe but which made it impossible to believe that our thinking was valid.

—C.S. Lewis

Everyone has a worldview (although you might not have realized it until reading the preceding paragraph). Your worldview explains why you see the world as you do, and why you act the way you do. Here is a simple example:

- Philosophy (what you believe): Suppose you believe in reincarnation.

- Worldview (when real-life situations are filtered through the grid of your philosophy): You won't stomp on a cockroach because it might be your departed great-grandfather.

Since philosophies shape your worldview, it is important to analyze how they affect your worldview before you swallow them hook, line, and sinker.

A Worldview with God at the Center

Let's see what your worldview might look like if your life philosophy is centered on what the Bible says about God.

- ***What about you?*** You are special (you always knew you were, but now you know why). God loves you. In fact, He allowed His Son, Jesus Christ, to die as the sacrifice for your sin. Your worldview will impact your sense of self-worth, and your actions will reflect that you are a fully devoted follower of Christ.

- **What about others?** They are special, too. Each person has worth and value because God loves them and because Christ died for them, too. This means that your behavior toward other people should be respectful. (You might even refrain from yelling at passing motorists who cut in front of you. It's a baby step, but it's a start.)

- **What about life?** There is meaning and purpose to life. All of life fits within God's plan. Your worldview will affect how you respond to issues such as abortion and euthanasia.

- **What about death?** You won't be afraid of death because you know that something better awaits you.

- **What about life after death?** The fact that every human being has a soul means we have an eternal nature. There is life after death. Your worldview will make you want to share the gospel message with other people so their eternity can be spent in heaven instead of hell.

- **What about truth?** Truth exists because God is truth. You read the Bible because your worldview compels you to learn of God's truth.

- **What about morality?** God has absolute standards of right and wrong. You try to conform your life to these standards because your worldview convinces you that there are consequences associated with right and wrong behavior.

- **What about the end of the world?** This life is just the beginning. The end of the world will mark the beginning of the rest of eternity. Your present life should be lived in a manner that reflects your expectation of what is yet to come.

If all of that description seems to be what you expected, that's because it fits with your worldview. But the perspectives would be very different if your worldview isn't centered on God.

A Worldview in Which There Is No God

Now let's see how different your worldview will be if you subscribe to the philosophy of naturalism:

- **What about you?** You are an accident—a random occurrence in the process of evolution. You have no significance in and of yourself. As artificial-intelligence guru Marvin Minsky said, "You are just a machine made out of meat." Suicide would not be outside your worldview because the loss of your life is a nonevent.

- **What about others?** If you are a randomly produced accident, then no one should care about you. And you shouldn't care about other people (because they are just the same). Since neither of you have any significance, you can use other people to your own benefit with no regard for them.

*S*o far as the eye of science can see, man is alone, absolutely alone, in a universe in which his very appearance is a kind of cosmic accident.

—John Herman Randall

- **What about life?** Life is without purpose and meaning. There is no grand plan. It all just happened by accident. Since life has no absolute value, abortion and euthanasia are just matters of personal preference and convenience. As Robert Wright wrote in *Time* magazine, "Children are just genetic conduits."

- **What about death?** Death brings the end of life. It's over. The final curtain. You've kicked the bucket. That's all, folks.

- **What about life after death?** Forget it! It's a fairy tale. So, with no eternal consequences, you can live in the present with absolutely no regard for life in the "ever after."

- *What about truth?* There is no truth, because there are no absolutes. Everything is relative. You can make up your own truth. Of course, you have to watch out for the people in power because they may impose the rules for their own version of the truth. So if you want to have things your own way, just put yourself in charge. (That's what Hitler did.)

- *What about morality?* Morality, smorality. Isn't this just a prudish concept imposed by a bunch of uptight, intolerant, judgmental religionists? Morality is whatever you agree that it should be. With no absolute boundaries, you can behave in whatever way you want. If someone else doesn't like your behavior, that should be of no consequence to you. There is no accountability to any higher power, so there is no concept of "sin." Live the way you want.

- *What about the end of the world?* Live for today because that's all there is.

We don't know about you, but this seems kind of depressing to us. (It also seems like the worldview that is promoted by most beer commercials.)

Christianity and Science Are Not Competing Worldviews

Stephen Hawking was asked if science and Christianity were competing worldviews. Knowing that Sir Isaac Newton had strong religious convictions, Hawking replied, "...then Newton would not have discovered the law of gravity." Naturalism and theism are competing worldviews, but religion and science are not.

What's Your Worldview?

Your worldview—how you respond to the circumstances and issues in the world around you—is determined by what you believe about how the world began. That's what makes the origins debate so important.

You shouldn't try to formulate a worldview by deciding each individual social issue on a case-by-case basis. (You won't live long enough, and you'll pop a few corpuscles in your cranium in the process.) Instead, decide what you believe about how the world began, and the rest will all fall into place.

The magnitude of the origins issue can be intimidating. But you don't have to master the disciplines of astrophysics, archaeology, molecular biology, microbiology, anthropology, and the rest. It is as simple as deciding between intelligent design or Darwinism, God versus no God.

Decide wisely. Your decision will determine what you do with the rest of your life.

"What's That Again?"

1. What you decide about how the world began will influence what you think about the ethical issues in your life.

2. Both sides of the origins debate have a Creation story. The Bible says that God created. The Darwinists say that the process of evolution created.

3. The scientific theory of Darwinism has led to naturalism becoming the prevailing cultural philosophy of our time. Naturalism is the conviction that nature is the only "force" in the universe, and that it is an impersonal force acting randomly and without plan or purpose.

4. The mainstream scientific community promotes naturalism as a philosophy. Because they intentionally refuse to consider God's existence, they won't even consider intelligent design as a possible theory.

5. Your personal philosophy is the foundation for your worldview. A worldview that includes God will cause you to recognize significance and accountability in life. A worldview without God may leave you without meaning or purpose.

6. Your worldview is determined by what you decide about how the world began: God, or no God.

Dig Deeper

We find the whole subject of worldview to be fascinating. And you probably do, too. Why shouldn't you? It's all about how you think and act. So we are pleased to recommend four great books that deal with worldview:

Our number-one recommendation for a book about worldview is *Reason in the Balance* by Phillip E. Johnson. In this book, Johnson explains how your views about cultural issues will be tainted if you unknowingly buy into the worldview of naturalism. If you only read one book on this list, read this one.

How Now Shall We Live? by Chuck Colson. This book isn't about origins in particular, although there are a few chapters that deal with these issues. The book is generally about understanding the Christian faith as an all-encompassing worldview.

Faith and Reason: Searching for a Rational Faith by Ronald H. Nash. There's not too much science in this book. Instead, it approaches faith in God from a philosophical perspective.

The Face That Demonstrates the Farce of Evolution by Hank Hanegraaff. This book exposes the deceptions of Darwinism that have been absorbed into our culture. It shows how our society has unwittingly bought into the naturalistic philosophy.

■ ■ ■

*Q*uestions for *R*eflection and *D*iscussion

1. From a Darwinist's perspective, tell the story of the beginnings of the universe and the origin of life on Earth.

2. From the intelligent design perspective, tell the story of how the universe came into existence and how life began on Earth.

3. Naturalism is the worldview philosophy that has developed from the Darwinist point of view. Explain what naturalism is all about.

4. Explain this statement: "What you decide about the origins of the universe will influence what you think about the ethical issues in your life." Give some examples.

5. Here is a thesis statement from this chapter: "What you decide about origins will influence what you think about what is going to happen when you die." Do you agree with it? What does it mean?

6. Explain why naturalism and a belief in God are competing worldviews, but why religion and science are not.

7. What are the ramifications of a worldview with God at the center?

8. What are the ramifications of a worldview in which there is no God?

■ ■ ■

Moving On...

We hope this book was helpful in clarifying the issues for you. If we helped you come to some conclusions, then that is great. If we just raised more questions in your mind, then we're happy about that as well (so long as you keep looking for the answers).

When you consider the evidence for the origins of life, ask yourself this question: Is there any evidence to suggest that an intelligent designer was involved in the process? If you answer that question in the affirmative, then you might want to investigate who that intelligent designer might be. After all, if there is an intelligent designer who planned it all, you ought to know as much as you can about the plan.

Index

The authors would enjoy hearing from you.
Contact them with your questions and comments,
or with requests to speak at an event:

Mail
Twelve Two Media
P.O. Box 25997
Fresno, CA 93729

E-mail
info@twelvetwomedia.com

Web site
www.twelvetwomedia.com

Exclusive Online Feature
Here's a study feature you're really going to like!
Simply go online at

www.christianity101online.com

There you will find a website designed exclusively for readers of *Creation and Evolution 101* and other books and Bible studies in the Christianity 101 series. When you log on to the site, just click on the book you are studying, and you will discover additional information, resources and helps, including

- *Background Material*—We can't put everything in this book, so this online section includes more material, and resources.

- *More Questions*—Do you need more questions for your group study? Here are additional questions for each chapter. Group leaders will find this section especially helpful.

- *Answers to Your Questions*—Do you have a question about something you read in this book? Post your question and an "online scholar" will respond.

- *FAQs*—In this section are answers to some of the most frequently asked questions about the topic you are studying.

What are you waiting for? Go online and become a part of the Christianity 101 community!

Christianity 101™ Bible Studies

Genesis: Discovering God's Answers to Life's Ultimate Questions
What did God have in mind when He started this world? What happened to His perfect design? Join Bruce and Stan in this exciting survey and learn how God's record of ancient times impacts *our* time.

John: Encountering Christ in a Life-Changing Way
John records how Jesus changed the lives of everyone He met. Bruce and Stan's fresh approach to these narratives will help you have your own personal, life-changing encounter with Jesus, the Son of God.

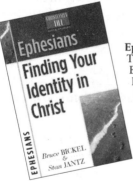

Ephesians: Finding Your Identity in Christ
This inviting little guide to the book of Ephesians gets straight to the heart of Paul's teaching on the believer's identity in Christ: We belong to Christ, the Holy Spirit is our guarantee, and we can share in God's power.

Revelation: Unlocking the Mysteries of the End Times
Just what is really going to happen? In this fascinating look at the apostle John's prophecy, Bruce and Stan demonstrate why—when God's involved—the end of the world is something to look forward to.

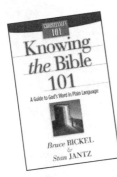

Knowing the Bible 101
A fresh approach to making Christianity understandable—even the hard parts! This user-friendly book relies on humor, insights, and relevant examples that will inspire readers not only to make sense of Scripture, but to *enjoy* Bible study.

Bruce & Stan's® *Guide Series:*

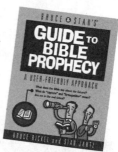

Bruce & Stan's® Guide to Bible Prophecy
Dealing with prophecy and end times in their witty, down-to-earth way, Bruce and Stan offer the Bible's answers to readers' big questions. Is the end really near? Who is the Antichrist? What is the Rapture?

Bruce & Stan's® Guide to Cults, Religions, and Spiritual Beliefs
"Here is our purpose, plain and simple: to provide an understandable overview of predominant religions and spiritual beliefs (with a little sense of humor thrown in along the way)." Clear explanations help readers understand the core issues of more than a dozen religions.

Bruce & Stan's® Guide to God
This fresh, user-friendly guide to the Christian life is designed to help new believers get started or recharge the batteries of believers of any age. Humorous subtitles, memorable icons, and learning aids present even difficult concepts in a simple way. Perfect for personal use or group study.

Bruce & Stan's® Pocket Guide Series:

Available from Harvest House Publishers:

Bruce & Stan's® Pocket Guide to Prayer
This very portable guide to prayer is as fun to read as it is uplifting. Readers will experience the wonder of communicating directly with God as Bruce and Stan explore the truth about how and why to pray.

Bruce & Stan's® Pocket Guide to Islam
Cutting through the mystery of Islam, Bruce and Stan's look at the world's second largest religion will help Christians better understand and witness to Muslims. Includes information about the Koran and Muslims' beliefs about Christ.

Available from Twelve Two Media:

To order these Pocket Guides,
visit www.twelvetwomedia.com

Bruce & Stan's® Pocket Guide to Knowing God's Will
Here, the wise and witty Bruce and Stan help readers discover the practical realities of hearing God, discerning His will, and walking in His perfect plan. Easy-to-understand explanations, highlighted with eye-catching graphics.

Bruce & Stan's® Pocket Guide to Knowing the Holy Spirit
The Holy Spirit often seems a most mysterious person. Bruce and Stan explore the many dimensions of His role in our lives. Covers "quenching the Spirit" and how to avoid it, and helpful ways to hear the Holy Spirit's voice.

Bruce & Stan's® Pocket Guide to Knowing Jesus
Using charts, sidebars, and information icons, this concise guide answers questions about Jesus and clarifies misconceptions about salvation, faith, and grace. Addresses the "all God, all-man" mystery, and the amazing truth of Christ's resurrection.

Bruce & Stan's® Pocket Guide to Sharing Your Faith
Great graphics and clear explanations make this guide easy to use. Readers will discover practical insights and ideas for confirming their own faith, handling objections about God and the Bible, and leading people to Jesus.

Bruce & Stan's® Pocket Guide to Studying Your Bible
Bruce and Stan cut through difficult concepts, unfamiliar customs and awkward names to make Bible study accessible and fun. Readers will explore Bible organization, translation differences, and effective ways to apply God's truths.